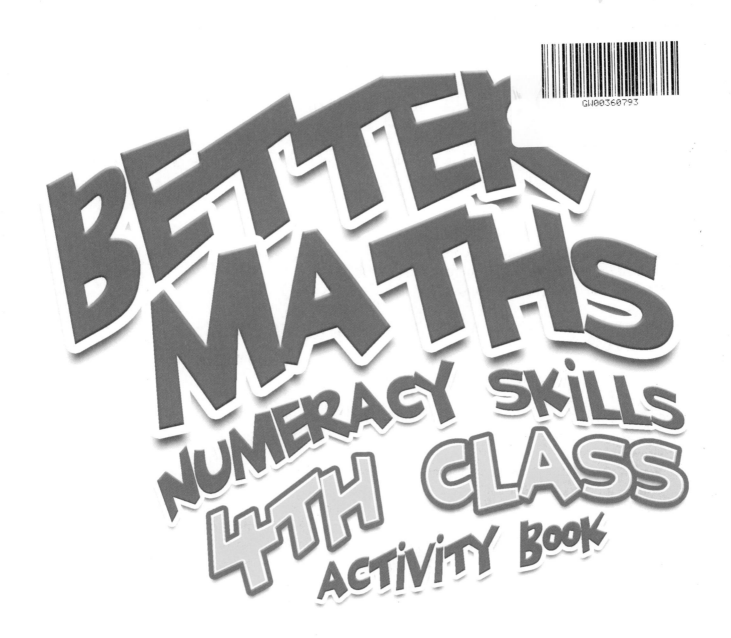

BETTER MATHS
NUMERACY SKILLS
4TH CLASS
ACTIVITY BOOK

educate.ie

Introduction

Better Maths is a series aimed at improving numeracy in primary schools. It is a sequenced, challenging and enjoyable programme covering all aspects of the Primary School Mathematics Curriculum. **Better Maths** uses contexts that connect mathematics to everyday experiences. It also provides opportunities to practise and perfect a range of mathematical skills. **Better Maths** includes a weekly assessment of pupil progress.

Features include:

- A comprehensive mathematics programme
- Systematic development and consolidation of numeracy skills
- Focused development of mathematical concepts
- Challenging, thought-provoking and enjoyable exercises
- Emphasis on understanding, reasoning and recalling
- Applying, integrating and implementing everyday mathematical problems
- Weekly assessments to challenge pupils
- Week-by-week pupil profiles as a guide for pupils, parents and teachers
- Online guidelines and materials for teachers

Better Maths 3rd Class and **Better Maths 4th Class** extend and build on the numeracy programme of the previous class level. The 3rd to 6th class books include a four-page, 30-unit pattern of work as follows:

- **Page 1 Quick Questions:** development of mental maths skills in numbers, fractions, decimals, shapes and space, measures and data
- **Page 2 Simply Sums:** computation exercises aimed at perfecting number work
- **Page 3 Problems:** challenging and enjoyable exercises connected to real-life mathematics
- **Page 4 Check-ups:** structured weekly assessments aimed at informing and motivating

Produced by

d(w)p

deirdre whelan *publishing*

Editor:	Ciara McNee
Design and layout:	Philip Ryan Graphic Design
Illustrations:	Sue King (*Plum Pudding*)

© 2014 Educate.ie, Castleisland, County Kerry, Ireland

ISBN: 978-1-909376-94-6

Printed in Ireland by Walsh Colour Print, Castleisland, County Kerry. Freephone 1800 613 111.

Acknowledgements

The author and publisher would like to thank the following for permission to reproduce photographs: Glow Images, Wikipedia Commons, Philip Ryan.

Contents

Unit 1 - Quick Questions

A Tables

1. $12 + 9 =$ `21`
2. $6 + 8 =$
3. $20 - 10 =$

4. $17 - 5 =$
5. $10 + 7 =$
6. $17 - 8 =$

7. $5 + 10 =$
8. $18 - 9 =$
9. $8 \times 4 =$

10. $6 \times 3 =$
11. $9 \times 5 =$
12. $7 \times 4 =$

B Calculate.

Always do work in brackets first.

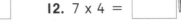

1. $10 +$ `26` $= 36$
2. $14 +$ `` $= 26$
3. $15 +$ `` $= 25$
4. $25 -$ `` $= 20$

5. $30 -$ `` $= 10$
6. $22 -$ `` $= 16$
7. $(4 \times 3) + 2 =$
8. $(6 \times 2) + 4 =$

9. $(12 \div 3) + 2 =$
10. $(9 \div 3) - 1 =$
11. `` $- 10 = 20$
12. `` $- 12 = 8$

C Numbers... Complete the sequences.

1. 14, 16, 18, `20`, `22`, `24`
2. 3, 7, 11, ___, ___, ___
3. 55, 44, 33, ___, ___, ___
4. 4, 8, 12, ___, ___, ___
5. 36, 30, 24, ___, ___, ___
6. 18, 15, 12, ___, ___, ___

7. 2, 5, 8, ___, ___, ___
8. 30, 25, 20, ___, ___, ___
9. 5, 10, 15, ___, ___, ___
10. 0·5, 1, 1·5, ___, ___, ___
11. 10, 20, 30, ___, ___, ___
12. 15, 30, 45, ___, ___, ___

D Money... How much change from €2·00?

1. Spent 66c and 43c. `91` c left.
2. Spent 49c and 35c. ___ c left.
3. Spent 37c and 82c. ___ c left.
4. Spent 20c and 19c. ___ c left.
5. Spent 99c and 94c. ___ c left.
6. Spent 24c and 57c. ___ c left.

7. Spent 95c and 23c. ___ c left.
8. Spent 10c and 66c. ___ c left.
9. Spent 43c and 80c. ___ c left.
10. Spent 62c and 65c. ___ c left.
11. Spent 78c and 29c. ___ c left.
12. Spent 24c and 69c. ___ c left.

E Figure it out. Tick (✓) the correct answer.

1. $39 - 10 + 4 =$ a 29 b 25 ✓ 33
2. $28 - 16 + 4 =$ a 16 b 12 c 18
3. $50 + 12 + 2 =$ a 64 b 36 c 62
4. $26 + 1 - 3 =$ a 22 b 24 c 30
5. $46 - 35 - 1 =$ a 11 b 10 c 9
6. $23 + 7 - 2 =$ a 26 b 28 c 24

7. $(4 \times 4) + 3 =$ a 15 b 17 c 19
8. $(5 \times 7) - 2 =$ a 31 b 33 c 35
9. $(15 \div 3) + 3 =$ a 8 b 18 c 17
10. $(9 \times 2) - 2 =$ a 16 b 18 c 20
11. $(24 \div 4) + 4 =$ a 12 b 10 c 8
12. $(7 \times 7) - 2 =$ a 33 b 47 c 45

A Work it out.

| 1. | 2 5 + 3 6 = **6 1** ✓ | 2. | 4 8 + 5 1 = **9 9** ✓ | 3. | 3 7 + 4 4 = **8X1** ✓ | 4. | 2 6 + 8 7 = **1 1 3** ✓ | 5. | 5 6 + 3 9 = **9 5** ✓ |

6. 4 5 / 6 2 / + 1 8 = **1 2 5** ✓
7. 5 5 / 3 7 / + 2 6 = **1 1 8**
8. 5 4 / 3 7 / + 2 9 = **1 0 0** ✓
9. 6 6 / 1 6 / + 2 8 = **1 1 9** x
10. 4 5 / 9 2 / + 9 9 = **1 5 6** ✓

11. 6 2 5 + 3 2 4 = **9 4 9** ✓
12. 3 2 3 + 1 1 8 = **4 4 1** ✓
13. 1 1 4 + 2 3 8 = **3 5 6** ✓
14. 4 8 7 − 2 3 6 = **7 6X3** ✓
15. 3 7 6 − 1 9 9 = **6 7 5**

16. 4·9 / 5·6 / + 2·4 = ~~crossed out~~
17. 7·8 / 9·3 / + 2·8 = **20·2**
18. 7·8 / 9·9 / + 3·4 =
19. 7·5 / 4·6 / + 2·7 =
20. 6·7 / 5·1 / + 2·8 =

B Work it out.

1. 5 1 5 3 − 2 7 3 = **3 8 0**
2. 3 4 3 7 − 2 8 6 = **1 5 1**
3. 1 2 0 1 − 1 9 9 = **0 1 5**
4. 6 7 9 − 3 8 3 =
5. 5 4 4 − 2 9 3 =

6. 1 4 3 / + 4 3 9 / − 2 6 5
7. 2 6 6 / + 1 0 7 / − 3 1 8
8. 4 2 7 / + 1 5 5 / − 2 6 9
9. 3 1 7 / + 1 4 5 / − 3 6 6
10. 4 1 6 / + 3 5 7 / − 2 9 9

11. €4·29 / €7·21 / + €8·33
12. €6·92 / €8·17 / + €10·32
13. €12·09 / €10·22 / + €4·63
14. €13·65 / €12·34 / + €5·18
15. €14·22 / €6·35 / + €7·47

16. 1 8 × 4
17. 2 5 × 5
18. 4 4 × 4
19. 2 4 × 3
20. 3 2 × 4

21. 1 7 × 3
22. 2 4 × 5
23. 8 2 × 3
24. 6 1 × 3
25. 3 5 × 3

Unit 1 - Problems

A Figure it out.

1. I have 34c, 22c and 10c. How much have I altogether? € `66`
2. I bought a pencil for 32c. What change did I get from 40c? € `12`
3. At school, I play from 8:50 to 8:55. How many mins do I play? `5` mins
4. I had a bag of 12 sweets but I ate $\frac{1}{2}$. How many have I left? `6`
5. Tom has a dog and two cats at home. How many legs in total have the pets? `20`
6. There are 14 crayons in a box. Half of them are red. How many are red? `7`
7. I was on page 13 of a book and I read 6 more pages. What page am I on now? `19`
8. Jill had €2·50 but spent 40c. How much money has she now? € `1`
9. Tom and John shared 22 toy animals. How many did each get? `11`
10. There are 13 boys and 9 girls in 4th class. How many pupils is that? `22`

B Think it out. Tick (✔) the correct answer.

1. Mum made two trays of 12 buns. How many buns is that? a 6 b 18 c✔ 24

2. 3 of 20 pupils in 4th class were sick. How many were at school? a 14 b✔ 17 c 23

3. What time is 10 mins before 8:00 a.m? a 7:10 a.m. b✔ 7:50 a.m. c 8:10 a.m.

4. Mary got 32c change from 50c. How much did she spend? a 8c b✔ 18c c 82c

5. How many 4s in 12? a✔ 3 b 4 c 6

6. Which shape has no corners? a triangle b✔ circle c rectangle

7. By how much is 27 greater than 19? a✔ 8 b 9 c 12

8. 23 + 14 + 14 = a 41 b 47 c✔ 51

9. What is missing? 12 + 10 < 11 + 11 a > b✔ < c =

10. Mary is 9 and Tim is 2 years younger. What age is Tim? a 2 b 7✔ c 11

C Puzzle it out. Use the 100-square to complete the tasks.

1. Write the missing numbers into the 100-square.
2. What number is 6 greater than 56? `NO`
3. What number is 9 less than 42? `Yes`
4. Complete the pattern.

   3, 6, 9, `12`, `15`, `18`, `21`, `24`, `27`

5. Complete the pattern.

   7, 17, 27, ☐, ☐, ☐, ☐, ☐, ☐

6. Count back in 7s. 49, 42, ☐, ☐, ☐, ☐

7. What number is halfway between 33 and 39? ☐

8. Ring all even numbers between 80 and 100.

9. Cross out all odd numbers between 54 and 64.

10. Write a sum that fits the answer: ☐ + ☐ = 34

1	2	3	4	5	6	7	8	9	10
11	12	13	14	15	16	17	18	19	20
21	22	23	24	25	26	27	28	29	30
31	32	33	34	35	36	37	38	39	40
41	42	43	44	45	46	47	48	49	50
51	52	53	54	55	56	57	58	59	60
61	62	63	64	65	66	67	68	69	70
71	72	73	74	75	76	77	78	79	80
81	82	83	84	85	86	87	88	89	90
91	92	93	94	95	96	97	98	99	100

Unit 1 - Check-up

A Tables

1. $3 + 8 =$ ☐
2. $6 + 8 =$ ☐
3. $3 + 12 =$ ☐
4. $12 - 3 =$ ☐
5. $16 - 7 =$ ☐
6. ☐ $- 9 = 5$
7. $17 -$ ☐ $= 9$
8. $4 \times 9 =$ ☐
9. $7 \times 4 =$ ☐
10. $9 \times$ ☐ $= 63$

Score ☐

B Computation

1.		7	3	8	2.			6	7	3.			4	9	4.	€4	5	·7	8	5.			3	7
	−	2	6	9		x			8				6	4		€2	3	·9	2		+		7	8
											+		8	7		+ €1	4	·3	6					
																					−		9	5

Give yourself 2 marks for each correct sum.

Score ☐

C Fractions and Decimals... Tick (✓) the correct answer.

1. $2·3 + 1·5 =$ [a] 2·8 [b] 3·5 [c] 3·8
2. $3·4 + 0·9 =$ [a] 4·3 [b] 4·5 [c] 4·7
3. $\frac{1}{2}$ of 34 $=$ [a] 17 [b] 39 [c] 68
4. $\frac{1}{4}$ of 40 $=$ [a] 4 [b] 8 [c] 10
5. $\frac{1}{3}$ of 18 $=$ [a] 3 [b] 6 [c] 9

6. $\frac{1}{3}$ of 18·6 $=$ [a] 3·2 [b] 6·2 [c] 9·2
7. $1·5 + 2 + 3·5 =$ [a] 5·5 [b] 6·5 [c] 7
8. $2 + 1·5 - 1 =$ [a] 2 [b] 2·5 [c] 3
9. $3·5 - 1 + 2·5 =$ [a] 4·5 [b] 5 [c] 5·5
10. $3·4 + 1·7 + 2 =$ [a] 4·3 [b] 6·6 [c] 7·1

Score ☐

D Shapes, Measures and Data... Show the times on the clocks.

1. 7:30	2. 5:35	3. 7:40	4. 9:05	5. 10:30
		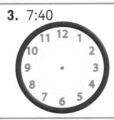	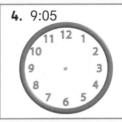	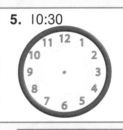

Give yourself 2 marks for each correct answer.

Score ☐

E Problem Solving

1. 23, 33 and 40 children are in school today. How many is that altogether? ☐

2. School ends at 2:10 p.m. Tom is home 10 minutes later. What time is that? ☐ : ☐ p.m.

3. 80 adults are on a train. Half of them are men. How many are women? ☐

4. Mum had €5·50 and gave half of it to Jane. How much did Jane get? € ☐

5. I bought milk for 55c. What change did I get from €1? € ☐

Give yourself 2 marks for each correct answer.

Score ☐

Unit 2 – Quick Questions

A Tables

1. 10 x 4 = ☐
2. 4 x 6 = ☐
3. 7 x 3 = ☐
4. 6 x 5 = ☐
5. 2 x 9 = ☐
6. 4 x 4 = ☐
7. 3 x 8 = ☐
8. 4 x 5 = ☐
9. 15 ÷ 3 = ☐
10. 21 ÷ 7 = ☐
11. 18 ÷ 9 = ☐
12. 28 ÷ 4 = ☐

B Calculate.

1. 23 + 33 = ☐
2. 64 – 21 = ☐
3. 12 + 102 = ☐
4. 25 + 27 = ☐
5. 433 – 23 = ☐
6. (11 x 7) + 1 = ☐
7. (36 ÷ 6) + 1 = ☐
8. 10 + 17 + 11 = ☐
9. 23 + 22 + 21 = ☐
10. 36 + 22 + 11 = ☐
11. 42 – ☐ = 31
12. ☐ – 11 = 34

C Numbers... Write the largest number or amount.

1. 459, 787, 695, 574 — 787
2. 945, 905, 950, 954 — ☐
3. 564, 237, 976, 265 — ☐
4. 365, 372, 354, 345 — ☐
5. €4·09, €4·59, €4·00, €4·80 — € ☐
6. €6·23, €6·55, €5·99, €5·94 — € ☐
7. €8·14, €4·18, €8·44, €4·89 — € ☐
8. €7·27, €6·33, €8·08, €7·99 — € ☐
9. 4·25, 5·5, 4·5, 5·25 — ☐
10. 2·25, 4·25, 3·25, 5·25 — ☐
11. 3·25, 3·52, 3·55, 3·22 — ☐
12. 7·63, 7·36, 3·76, 6·76 — ☐

D Time... Show the times on the clocks.

1. 1:25
3. 12:40
5. 12:05
7. 6:30
9. 3:20

2. 5:35
4. 2:55
6. 4:15
8. 9:00
10. 5:10

E Figure it out. Use +, – or X to complete the number sentences.

1. 3 ☐+☐ 10 ☐+☐ 8 = 21
2. 14 ☐ 4 ☐ 6 = 16
3. 12 ☐ 4 ☐ 3 = 11
4. 6 ☐ 2 ☐ 12 = 16
5. €2·55 ☐ €1·45 = €1·10
6. €1·50 ☐ €1·45 = €2·95
7. 4 ☐ 2 ☐ 2 = 8
8. 3 ☐ $\frac{1}{2}$ = $2\frac{1}{2}$
9. (4 ☐ 3) ☐ 1 = 11
10. (5 ☐ 2) ☐ 3 = 13
11. (6 ☐ 3) ☐ 1 = 17
12. (12 ☐ 1) ☐ 2 = 22

A Work it out.

1.
```
    4  6
+   8  7
_____
```

2.
```
    3  7
+   3  6
_____
```

3.
```
    2  6
+   5  3
_____
```

4.
```
    4  8
+   2  7
_____
```

5.
```
    2  8
+   9  0
_____
```

6.
```
    3  6
    4  2
+   1  4
_____
```

7.
```
    5  4
    3  4
+   2  2
_____
```

8.
```
    2  9
    1  1
+   4  9
_____
```

9.
```
    5  6
    1  6
+   2  3
_____
```

10.
```
    7  8
    2  5
+   9  4
_____
```

11.
```
    5  9  7
+   4  2  7
_____
```

12.
```
    3  4  2
+   4  1  5
_____
```

13.
```
    5  4  1
-   2  6  6
_____
```

14.
```
    4  2  7
-   1  4  9
_____
```

15.
```
    4  7  8
-   2  9  9
_____
```

16.
```
    2  3
x      6
_____
```

17.
```
    5  5
x      4
_____
```

18.
```
    2  4
x      9
_____
```

19.
```
    1  4
x      8
_____
```

20.
```
    4  6
x      4
_____
```

B Work it out.

1.
```
    2  8  6
-   2  4  8
_____
```

2.
```
    3  6  5
-   2  3  6
_____
```

3.
```
    5  2  3
-   3  1  4
_____
```

4.
```
    8  1  9
-   2  2  3
_____
```

5.
```
    6  0  7
-   2  7  8
_____
```

6.
```
    3  6  6
+   2  8  7
_____
-   4  0  7
_____
```

7.
```
    5  1  8
+   3  2  8
_____
-   4  2  9
_____
```

8.
```
    3  2  9
+   4  3  7
_____
-   5  5  5
_____
```

9.
```
    2  6  6
+   1  5  7
_____
-   3  4  7
_____
```

10.
```
    5  0  3
+   4  5  5
_____
-   2  6  7
_____
```

11.
```
    €1 ·8  2
    €4 ·4  0
+   €2 ·2  9
_____
```

12.
```
    €5 ·0  6
    €2 ·4  9
+   €1 ·6  4
_____
```

13.
```
    €2 ·3  4
    €3 ·1  9
+   €3 ·9  9
_____
```

14.
```
    €4 ·1  6
    €3 ·8  5
+   €1 ·1  6
_____
```

15.
```
    €3 ·2  7
    €2 ·2  9
+   €2 ·4  9
_____
```

16.
```
    4  5
x      7
_____
```

17.
```
    6  4
x      5
_____
```

18.
```
    3  7
x      6
_____
```

19.
```
    7  8
x      5
_____
```

20.
```
    7  7
x      7
_____
```

21.
```
    2  7
x      9
_____
```

22.
```
    5  4
x      5
_____
```

23.
```
    2  9
x      4
_____
```

24.
```
    1  8
x      4
_____
```

25.
```
    4  4
x      6
_____
```

Unit 2 - Problems

A Figure it out.

Tom has 10 coloured pencils.

1. 3 pencils are orange. How many are not orange? 7 ✓
2. 2 pencils are blue. How many are not blue or orange? 8 ✓
3. Tom has as many red pencils as blue pencils. How many pencils are red? 2 ✓
4. How many pencils are not orange or blue or red?
5. He has two more orange pencils than green. How many are green? 3
6. How many pencils are orange, blue, red or green?
7. The rest of the pencils are yellow. How many are yellow? 0
8. Tom gave $\frac{1}{2}$ the pencils to Paul. How many did Paul get? 5
9. The pencils are 20c each. How many can Tom buy for €1·00? 5
10. Paul spent 60c on pencils. How many did he buy? 3

Colour Tom's pencils.

B Think it out. Tick (✓) the correct answer.

1. Eight hundred and forty-six =
   a 864   b 468   c 846 ✓

2. How many 50c in €5·00?   a 5   b 10 ✓   c 50

3. Add three 20c and four 50c.
   a €2·60 ✓   b €2·10   c €0·70

4. There are 34 boys and 45 girls in a school.
   How many is that?   a 49   b 79 ✓   c 88

5. Twin babies are the same weight, and
   weigh 15 kg in total. How much does one
   baby weigh?   a 1·5 kg   b 7·5 kg ✓   c 30 kg

6. The side of a square is 3 cm long. What is
   the total length of all sides?
   a 6 cm   b 9 cm   c 12 cm ✓

7. A soccer team has 11 players. How many
   are on 2 teams?   a 13   b 22   c 24

8. What is $\frac{1}{2}$ of 10 plus $\frac{1}{2}$ of 20?
   a 5   b 10   c 15

9. 22 − 10 ∠ 4 + 9   a <   b =   c >

10. How many legs altogether do 9 people
    have?   a 18   b 11   c 7

C Puzzle it out. Do the sums and complete the cross-number puzzle.

If you need to, you can work out these sums in your copy.

Across
1. 1512 − 588 = 924
3. 400 − 253 = 147
6. 314 − 72 = 242
8. 102 + 88 =
9. 802 − 126 = 676
10. 10 × 9 = 90
11. 6512 − 588 = 924
13. 392 − 162 = 230
15. 1150 + 702 = 34
16. 1004 + 1112 = 892

Down
1. 5421 + 4088 =
2. 918 − 512 =
3. 512 − 336 =
4. 5512 + 1588 = 710
5. 4045 − 2040 = 2005
7. 1342 + 2702 = 4044
12. 53 × 5 = 305
14. 146 + 155 =

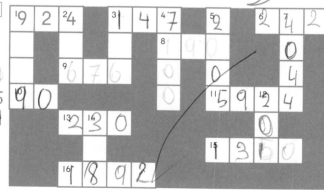

Unit 2 - Check-up

A Tables

1. $8 + 6 = \boxed{14}$
2. $\boxed{7} + 8 = 15$
3. $8 + \boxed{\cancel{11}} = 17$

4. $15 - \boxed{9} = 6$
5. $17 - \boxed{\cancel{11}} = 8$
6. $\boxed{} - 6 = 9$

7. $3 \times 7 = \boxed{21}$
8. $\boxed{5} \times 8 = 40$
9. $48 \div \boxed{8} = 6$

10. $27 \div 3 = \boxed{9}$

Score [ ]

B Computation

1.		4	5
	1	5	6
+	1	2	7
	2	2	8

2.	1	$\cancel{2}^9$	$\cancel{9}^1$	0
	–	2	4	6
		1	5	4

3.		8	4
	x	2	5
	4	2	0

4.	€3	7	·2	4
+	€5	6	·2	9
–	€1	0	·4	8

5.		3	7
	x	4	6
	2	2	9
–		9	6
			3

Give yourself 2 marks for each correct sum.

Score [ ]

C Fractions and Decimals

1. $\frac{1}{3}$ of 66 = $\boxed{18}$
2. $\frac{1}{4}$ of 24 = $\boxed{3}$
3. $\frac{1}{3}$ of 36 = $\boxed{12}$
4. $3·2 + 0·3 = \boxed{3,5}$
5. $3·5 - 1 + 0·5 = \boxed{2.9}$

6. $2·3 + 1·5 + 1·1 = \boxed{}$
7. $1·5 + 1·5 + 1 = \boxed{}$
8. $\frac{1}{4}$ of 12 plus $\frac{1}{3}$ of 12 = $\boxed{}$
9. $\frac{1}{3}$ of 18 less $\frac{1}{2}$ of 8 = $\boxed{}$
10. $\frac{1}{4}$ of 4 plus $\frac{1}{3}$ of 6 = $\boxed{}$

Score [ ]

D Shapes, Measures and Data

How much change will I have from €10·00 if I spend:

1. €2·07 and €1·66? € [ ]
2. €3·03 and €0·89? € [ ]

Which measure is used (litres, metres or grams) for:

3. distance? meters
4. liquid? liters
5. weight? grams

Give yourself 2 marks for each correct answer.

Score [ ]

E Problem Solving... Tick (✓) the correct answer.

1. How many 2s in 14? ✓ 7 | b 12 | c 28
2. How many sides in a square? a 2 | b 3 | ✓ 4
3. By how much is 67 greater than 58? ✓ 9 | b 10 | c 11
4. What is missing? $12 - \boxed{} = 5$ | a 5 | ✓ 7 | c 17
5. How much for 3 apples at 40c each? a 43c | b 70c | ✓ €1·20

58

40
40
40

20 19 18 17 16 15 14 13 12 11 10 9 8 7 6 5 4 3 2 1

Give yourself 2 marks for each correct answer.

Score [ ]

Unit 3 - Quick Questions

A Tables

1. 10 + 6 = $\boxed{16}$
2. 4 + 5 = $\boxed{9}$
3. 16 − 8 = $\boxed{8}$
4. 16 − 7 = $\boxed{9}$
5. 10 + 8 = $\boxed{18}$
6. 9 x 5 = $\boxed{45}$
7. 8 x 6 = $\boxed{48}$
8. 5 x 7 = $\boxed{35}$
9. 30 ÷ 3 = $\boxed{10}$
10. 81 ÷ 9 = $\boxed{9}$
11. 72 ÷ 8 = $\boxed{9}$
12. 54 ÷ 6 = $\boxed{9}$

B Calculate.

1. 24 + 35 = $\boxed{59}$
2. 35 − 24 = $\boxed{11}$ 120
3. 100 + 44 − 20 = $\boxed{}$
4. 211 + 22 + $\boxed{189}$ = 235
5. 68 − 22 = $\boxed{}$
6. (12 x 3) + 4 = $\boxed{}$
7. (33 ÷ 3) + 5 = $\boxed{}$
8. €1·44 + €1·44 = €$\boxed{}$
9. 2·5 + 1 = $\boxed{}$
10. 3·5 − 1 = $\boxed{}$
11. 45 − $\boxed{}$ = 32
12. $\boxed{}$ − 11 = 25

C Numbers... Are these numbers > (greater than) or < (less than) each other?

1. 43 $\boxed{<}$ 45
2. 127 $\boxed{>}$ 111
3. 762 $\boxed{>}$ 522
4. 33 + 44 $\boxed{<}$ 80
5. 33 x 3 $\boxed{>}$ 100
6. 11 x 3 $\boxed{33}$ 30
7. 20 + 10 + 10 $\boxed{>}$ 50
8. €43·40 $\boxed{}$ €4·34
9. 0·5 $\boxed{}$ 0·25
10. 1·5 $\boxed{>}$ 0·25
11. €1·81 $\boxed{<}$ €1·18
12. €2·96 $\boxed{<}$ €2·69

83 50
60 83
90 33
    33
    45
    1·45
    50 9
    50
    28

D Money... Find the cost of each shopping list.

Copy (C) = 50c   Pencil (P) = 33c   Biro (B) = 45c

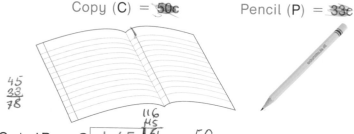

1. 2C + 1B = €$\boxed{1·45}$
2. 1C + 1P + 2B = €$\boxed{}$
3. 1C + 2P + 1B = €$\boxed{1·61}$
4. 2C + 1P + 2B = €$\boxed{1·78}$
5. 1C + 1P + 1B = €$\boxed{1·61}$
6. 2C + 1P + 1B = €$\boxed{1·61}$
7. 3C + 1P + 2B = €$\boxed{2·73}$
8. 4C + 2P = €$\boxed{2·90}$
9. 3C + 3P = €$\boxed{1·49}$
10. 1C + 3P + 2B = €$\boxed{}$
11. 3C + 1P = €$\boxed{}$
12. 4C + 3P = €$\boxed{}$

45
33
78

116
45
161

50c

50c 66c 45c

1·50
45
145
173

50
33
33
33
149

50
50
50

E Figure it out. True (✓) or false (✗)?

1. 84 is divisible by 4. $\boxed{✓}$
2. 52 is half of 102. $\boxed{✗}$
3. $\frac{1}{2}$ of 224 is 112. $\boxed{✓}$
4. $\frac{1}{4}$ of 40 is 4. $\boxed{✗}$
5. 96 is a multiple of 6. $\boxed{}$
6. 2:00 p.m. is morning time. $\boxed{}$

> A **multiple** is a number that can be divided by another number without leaving a remainder. 15 is a multiple of 5.

7. A triangle has 3 sides. $\boxed{}$
8. $2\frac{1}{2}$ is greater than 2. $\boxed{}$
9. $1\frac{1}{2} + 1\frac{1}{2} = 4$ $\boxed{}$
10. 655 > 677 $\boxed{}$
11. A quarter of 16 is 6. $\boxed{}$
12. €2·30 − €0·99 = €1·31 $\boxed{}$

Top margin (handwritten working):
$$33 \times 3 = 66$$

A — Work it out.

1. $76 + 47 = 123$
2. $94 + 27 = 121$
3. $65 + 36 = 101$
4. $88 + 47 = 135$
5. $95 + 36 = 131$

6. $73 + 26 + 33 = 132$
7. $64 + 56 + 38 = 158$
8. $56 + 43 + 59 = 158$
9. $28 + 36 + 43 = 107$
10. $89 + 69 + 39 = 197$

11. $476 + 238 = 714$
12. $176 + 266 = 442$
13. $563 + 419 = 982$
14. $312 - 97 = 235$
15. $526 - 176 = 350$

16. $78 \times 4 = 312$
17. $62 \times 5 = 310$
18. $51 \times 7 = 357$
19. $38 \times 4 = 122$
20. $65 \times 8 = 520$

B — Work it out.

1. $734 - 253 = 481$
2. $634 - 76 = 558$
3. $321 - 114 = 207$
4. $326 - 277 = 049$
5. $407 - 128 = 279$

6. $377 + 276 = 653; \; 653 - 508 = 145$
7. $416 + 199 = 615; \; 615 - 555 = 060$
8. $414 + 166 = 580; \; 580 - 325 = 255$
9. $488 + 378 = 866; \; 866 - 499 = 065$
10. $187 + 357 = 544; \; 544 - 476 = 058$

11. €4.25 + €1.28 + €3.37 = €9.20
12. €3.29 + €3.88 + €2.06 = €9.93
13. €2.11 + €4.08 + €3.73 = €9.92
14. €2.37 + €4.17 + €2.85 = €9.39
15. €3.91 + €4.19 + €1.63 = €7.73

16. $63 \times 5 = 385$
17. $76 \times 6 = 456$
18. $24 \times 7 = 168$
19. $55 \times 6 = 330$
20. $67 \times 5 = 335$

21. $13.5 + 25.6 + 20.9 = 59.9$
22. $14.4 + 23.6 + 23.7 = 63.7$
23. $11.4 + 15.8 + 20.4 = 47.6$
24. $24.4 + 15.5 + 12.7 = 52.6$
25. $12.9 + 9.6 + 17.4 = 38.9$

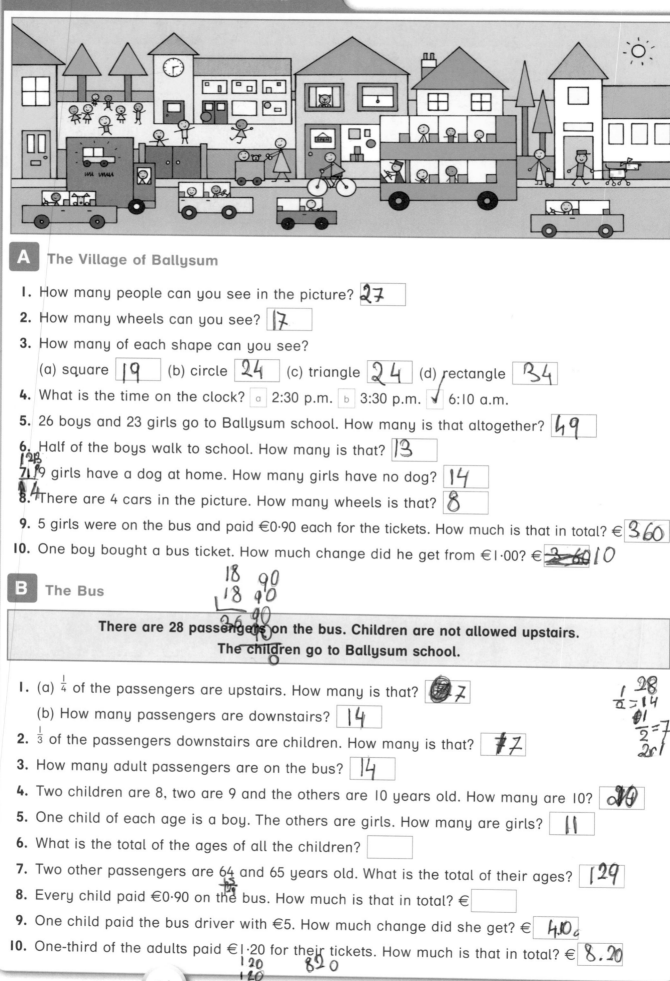

A The Village of Ballysum

1. How many people can you see in the picture? 27

2. How many wheels can you see? 17

3. How many of each shape can you see?

   (a) square 19   (b) circle 24   (c) triangle 24   (d) rectangle 34

4. What is the time on the clock? a 2:30 p.m.   b 3:30 p.m. ✓ 6:10 a.m.

5. 26 boys and 23 girls go to Ballysum school. How many is that altogether? 49

6. Half of the boys walk to school. How many is that? 13

7. 9 girls have a dog at home. How many girls have no dog? 14

8. There are 4 cars in the picture. How many wheels is that? 8

9. 5 girls were on the bus and paid €0·90 each for the tickets. How much is that in total? € 360

10. One boy bought a bus ticket. How much change did he get from €1·00? € ~~2 60~~ 10

B The Bus

18 90
18 90
26 90
10

There are 28 passengers on the bus. Children are not allowed upstairs.
The children go to Ballysum school.

1. (a) $\frac{1}{4}$ of the passengers are upstairs. How many is that? ~~7~~

   (b) How many passengers are downstairs? 14

2. $\frac{1}{3}$ of the passengers downstairs are children. How many is that? ~~7~~ 7

3. How many adult passengers are on the bus? 14

4. Two children are 8, two are 9 and the others are 10 years old. How many are 10? ~~20~~

5. One child of each age is a boy. The others are girls. How many are girls? 11

6. What is the total of the ages of all the children?

7. Two other passengers are 64 and 65 years old. What is the total of their ages? 129

8. Every child paid €0·90 on the bus. How much is that in total? €

9. One child paid the bus driver with €5. How much change did she get? € 4.10

10. One-third of the adults paid €1·20 for their tickets. How much is that in total? € 8.20

$\frac{1}{4} = \frac{28}{14}$
$\frac{1}{2} = 7$

120
120
120
120
120

820

Unit 3 - Check-up

A Tables

1. 5 + ☐ = 12
4. 13 – ☐ = 8
7. 5 x 9 = ☐
10. 72 ÷ 9 = ☐

2. ☐ + 5 = 16
5. 20 – ☐ = 11
8. ☐ x 8 = 64

3. 10 + ☐ = 19
6. ☐ – 10 = 11
9. 40 ÷ ☐ = 8

Score ☐

B Computation

1.		2	0	8
		3	8	8
	+	2	6	9

2.	4	6	4
	x		6

3.		m	cm
		6	3	4
		5	4	8
	+	8	3	9

4.	€9	·2	3
–	€8	·9	9
x			3

5.		3	7	2
	+	1	7	8
	–	2	9	5

Give yourself 2 marks for each correct sum.

Score ☐

C Fractions and Decimals… Shade the correct amount of each shape.

1. $\frac{1}{3}$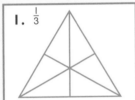

3. 0·5

5. 0·1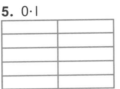

7. $\frac{1}{3}$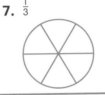

9. $\frac{3}{8}$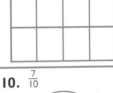

2. 0·6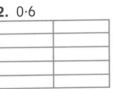

4. 0·5

6. $\frac{1}{4}$

8. $\frac{1}{4}$

10. $\frac{7}{10}$

Score ☐

D Shapes, Measures and Data… Write **speed**, **distance**, **greater than**, **less than** or **length**.

1. _____
2. _____
3. _____
4. _____
5. _____

Give yourself 2 marks for each correct answer.

Score ☐

E Problem Solving

Half of the 24 children in 4th class are boys. Half the boys have blue eyes. 7 girls have blue eyes. One-quarter of the girls have brown eyes. The other girls have green eyes.

1. How many girls are in 4th class? ☐

2. How many boys have blue eyes? ☐

3. How many boys and girls have blue eyes? ☐

4. How many girls have brown eyes? ☐

5. How many girls have green eyes? ☐

Give yourself 2 marks for each correct answer.

Score ☐

15

A Tables

1. 12 + 7 = ☐
2. 17 – 9 = ☐
3. 3 x 9 = ☐
4. 18 – ☐ = 8
5. 10 – ☐ = 7
6. 4 x 7 = ☐
7. 9 x 3 = ☐
8. 4 x 9 = ☐
9. 21 ÷ 3 = ☐
10. 49 ÷ 7 = ☐
11. 18 ÷ 9 = ☐
12. 48 ÷ 6 = ☐

B Calculate.

1. 10 + 13 + 14 = 37
2. 35 – 24 = 11
3. 22 + 33 + 44 = 99
4. 5 + 15 = 20
5. 20 – 10 = 10
6. 23 + 13 + 12 = 48
7. 3 + 3 + 3 + 3 = 12
8. 2 + 2 + 2 + 2 + 2 = 10
9. 43 + 54 = 97
10. 90 – 15 = 75
11. 60 – 50 = 10
12. ☐ – 15 = 20

C Numbers... Are these numbers $>$ (greater than) or $<$ (less than) each other?

1. 67 > 65
2. 45 < 54
3. 637 < 565
4. 879 > 897
5. 22 x 3 > 50
6. 11 x 6 < 660
7. 12 + 8 + 20 < 45
8. 15 + 10 < 30 + 30
9. 2·5 ☐ 2·35
10. 0·25 ☐ 0·5
11. €5·20 > €5·02
12. €2·43 < €3·24

D Money... Write as euros and cents.

1. 932c € 9·32
2. 406c € ▨▨
3. 200c € ▨▨
4. 87c € ▨▨
5. 426c € ▨▨
6. 147c € ☐
7. 316c € ☐
8. 510c € ☐
9. 601c € ☐
10. 311c € ☐
11. 101c € ☐
12. 17c € ☐

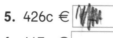

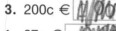

E Figure it out. Tick (✓) the correct answer.

1. (4 x 3) + 7 =   a 17   b 19   ✓c 21
2. (21 ÷ 3) + 4 =   a 7   b 9   ✓ 11
3. (6 x 5) – 7 =   a 21   ✓b 23   c 25
4. (36 ÷ 3) – 4 =   28   a 8   ✓b 12   c 14
5. (2 x 3) + 2 =   +12 / 40   a 8   b 6   c 10
6. €2·30 – €0·99 + €1·20 =   a €2·51   b €3·29   c €3·50
7. (€4·99 – €3·49) x 2 =   a €2·99   b €3   c €3·50
8. 3 m 06 cm =   a 36 cm   b 306 cm   c 3006 cm
9. 3 m 06 cm + 4 m 99 cm =   a 794 cm   b 799 cm   c 805 cm
10. $\frac{1}{3}$ of 54 =   a 17   b 18   c 19
11. 23 + 7 – 11 =   a 31   b 15   c 19
12. 35 + 6 – 3 =   a 41   b 38   c 35

A Work it out.

1.	2.	3.	4.	5.
34 x 4	24 x 3	32 x 5	61 x 8	56 x 6

6.	7.	8.	9.	10.
37 26 + 88	67 16 + 68	54 26 + 33	49 6 + 99	67 83 + 46

11.	12.	13.	14.	15.
467 388 + 177	366 527 + 46	216 59 + 146	76 97 + 706	416 267 + 94

16.	17.	18.	19.	20.
824 − 417	897 − 396	563 − 276	456 − 274	408 − 199

B Work it out.

1.	2.	3.	4.	5.
3 ⟌ 633	4 ⟌ 804	2 ⟌ 468	3 ⟌ 906	4 ⟌ 844

6.	7.	8.	9.	10.
€34·78 + €26·44 − €19·86	€25·66 + €23·19 − €37·49	€45·23 + €17·38 − €24·86	€28·35 + €27·47 − €33·99	€37·58 + €17·06 − €20·74

11. m cm	12. m cm	13. m cm	14. m cm	15. m cm
1 76 1 40 + 2 80	1 70 2 44 + 1 65	3 12 1 39 + 1 10	1 42 3 9 + 1 18	1 85 1 97 + 2 40

16.	17.	18.	19.	20.
27 x 8	34 x 6	48 x 7	26 x 3	35 x 7

21.	22.	23.	24.	25.
46 x 8	67 x 3	73 x 5	87 x 7	93 x 8

Unit 4 – Problems

A Figure it out.

1. 36 passengers were on a bus. 14 were upstairs.
   How many were downstairs? **22**

2. Apples are 15c each. How much for 4 apples? € **6.00**

3. Tom had €2·00. He spent €1·20. How much has he left? € **1.50**

4. Jenny had 18 jellies and shared them with Kate and Úna. How many did each get? **6**

5. The farmer had 21 sheep. He sold 5 and bought 2 more. How many has he now? **19**

6. 12 children ate 2 apples each. How many apples in total was that? **24**

7. Stamps are 60c each. How many stamps can you buy for €2·20? **9**

8. Jim arrived at school 15 mins late at 9:15 a.m. What time does school start? **9:00**

9. A farmer has 12 chickens. How many wings in total on the chickens? **24**

10. Tom is 2 years older than Pete. Together their age is 18. What age is Pete? **16**

B Think it out. Tick (✓) the correct answer.

1. Úna has 5 more crayons than Tom. Tom has 6. Úna has a 1 ✓ 11 c 56

2. A school has 112 pupils. How many more than 100 is that? ✓ 12 b 100 c 212

3. School starts at 8:30 a.m. John arrived 10 mins early at
   a 8:50 a.m. b 8:40 a.m. c✓ 8:20 a.m.

4. I bought 6 sausages for 60c. How much for 1 sausage? a 6c ✓ 10c c 66c

5. How many 10s in 74? a 6 ✓ 7 c 8

6. How many angles in a triangle?
   ✓ 3 b 4 c 6

7. By how much is 234 greater than 134?
   ✓ 100 b 110 c 10

8. A farmer had 89 sheep and lost 11. She now has a 888 b 79 ✓ 78

9. What is missing? 24 − 12 ✓ 5 + 5
   a > ✓ < c =

10. Twins and a baby are 9 in total. The baby is 1. The twins are a 4 b 6 ✓ 8

C Puzzle it out. Complete the Sudokus using 1, 2, 3 and 4 in each square, row and column.

Remember! Use each number only once in each square, row and column.

1.

1	2	3	4
3	4	1	2
2	1	4	3
4	3	2	1

2.

2	3	4	1
4	1	3	2
1	2	1	2
3	4	4	3

3.

2	1	3	4
3	4	1	2
1	4	1	3
3	2	4	2

18

Unit 4 - Check-up

A Tables

1. $8 + 7 = \boxed{}$ 4. $17 - 9 = \boxed{}$ 7. $18 - \boxed{} = 9$ 10. $7 \times \boxed{} = 56$

2. $9 + 4 = \boxed{}$ 5. $13 - 4 = \boxed{}$ 8. $7 \times 9 = \boxed{}$

3. $4 + \boxed{} = 13$ 6. $\boxed{} - 7 = 6$ 9. $9 \times 4 = \boxed{}$

Score $\boxed{}$

B Computation

1.		5	0	2.		5	8	3.		9		4.	€2	9	·0	4	5.			4	7
	−		7		×		6				8		€1	0	·6	7		+		6	9
		2	4	2					+	3	8		+	€8	·9	6					
									1	5	9							−		8	8

Give yourself 2 marks for each correct sum. **Score** $\boxed{}$

C Fractions and Decimals... Tick (✓) the correct answer.

1. $6·7 + 2·3 =$ a 8·4 b 8·9 c 9   6. $0·5 + 1·5 + 2 =$ a 2·5 b 3·5 c 4

2. $5·2 + 0·4 =$ a 4·8 b 5·6 c 9·2   7. $3 + 1·5 + 1·5 =$ a 5·5 b 6 c 6·5

3. $\frac{1}{4}$ of $44 =$ a 4 b 11 c 22   8. $4·5 + 2 - 1·5 =$ a 5 b 6·5 c 8

4. $\frac{1}{10}$ of $100 =$ a 1 b 10 c 50   9. $2·9 + 1·4 - 1 =$ a 3·3 b 4·2 c 5·3

5. $\frac{1}{6}$ of $12 =$ a 2 b 3 c 6   10. $2 + 2·7 - 1·5 =$ a 3·2 b 4·2 c 6·2

Score $\boxed{}$

D Shapes, Measures and Data

How much is left from 1 litre of milk if I drink:

1. 750 ml? ml

2. 400 ml? $\boxed{}$ ml

Which measure is greater:

3. gram or kilogram? $\boxed{}$

4. litre or millilitre? $\boxed{}$

5. metre or centimetre? $\boxed{}$

Give yourself 2 marks for each correct answer. **Score** $\boxed{}$

E Problem Solving

1. Jill bought 3 bars for €3·00. Two were €0·90 and €1·30. How much was the third? € 1.80

2. Mary has 3 dogs and 2 cats. How many legs have all the animals? 20

3. Joe ran a race in 35 minutes. He started at 10:00 a.m. When did he finish? 10:35 a.m.

4. Dad shared €2·10 among his 3 children. How much did each child get? € 1

5. John lives 2 km from school; Mary lives twice as far away. How far away is Mary? 4 km

Give yourself 2 marks for each correct answer. **Score** $\boxed{}$

Unit 5 - Quick Questions

A Tables

1. 5 + 9 =
2. 8 + 5 =
3. 17 − 9 =

4. 16 − 7 =
5. 6 + 8 =
6. 6 x 9 =

7. 4 x 12 =
8. 5 x 12 =
9. 36 ÷ 3 =

10. 60 ÷ 6 =
11. 54 ÷ 9 =
12. 49 ÷ 7 =

B Calculate.

1. 15 + ☐ + 1 = 32
2. 35 + ☐ = 47
3. 70 + ☐ = 96
4. 65 − ☐ = 32

5. 45 − ☐ = 23
6. 66 − ☐ = 35
7. (5 x 2) + 8 = ☐
8. (4 x 6) + 3 = ☐

9. 43 + 54 = ☐
10. (6 ÷ 3) + 10 = ☐
11. 30 − ☐ + 5 = 10
12. 20 + ☐ − 15 = 8

C Numbers... Complete the sequences.

1. 4, 10, 16, ☐, ☐, ☐
2. 5, 9, 13, ☐, ☐, ☐
3. 63, 54, 45, ☐, ☐, ☐
4. 6, 12, 18, ☐, ☐, ☐
5. 40, 35, 30, ☐, ☐, ☐
6. 36, 30, 24, ☐, ☐, ☐

7. 7, 12, 17, ☐, ☐, ☐
8. 45, 39, 33, ☐, ☐, ☐
9. 3·5, 4, 4·5, ☐, ☐, ☐
10. 7·5, 6·5, 5·5, ☐, ☐, ☐
11. 1·5, 2, 2·5, ☐, ☐, ☐
12. 9·5, 9, 8·5, ☐, ☐, ☐

D Time... Write the digital times.

1. 6:45
2. :
3. :
4. :
5. :
6. :
7. :
8. :
9. :
10. :

E Figure it out. Use +, −, x or ÷ to complete the number sentences.

1. 2 ☐ 4 ☐ 2 = 16
2. 32 ☐ 4 = 8
3. 2 ☐ 3 ☐ 2 = 12
4. (8 ☐ 4) ☐ 3 = 12

5. €3·50 ☐ 2 = €7·00
6. €5·50 ☐ €2·34 = €3·16
7. 2·5 ☐ 2 ☐ 1·5 = 6
8. 3·5 ☐ 1·5 ☐ 1 = 4

9. (6 ☐ 2) ☐ 6 = 18
10. 5 ☐ 5 ☐ 6 = 4
11. (2 ☐ 4) ☐ 10 = 80
12. (10 ☐ 6) ☐ 2 = 8

20

A Work it out.

1.	2.	3.	4.	5.
65 x 4	28 x 6	34 x 9	26 x 7	65 x 5

6.	7.	8.	9.	10.
406 329 + 88	167 64 + 368	554 56 + 43	171 65 + 198	467 396 + 326

11.	12.	13.	14.	15.
456 511 + 72	453 712 + 156	299 24 + 146	556 877 + 4	307 283 + 69

16.	17.	18.	19.	20.
723 − 115	512 − 346	49 x 4	56 x 7	29 x 3

B Work it out.

1.	2.	3.	4.	5.
3)3 3 6	4)3 3 6	2)3 3 6	6)3 3 6	8)3 3 6

6.	7.	8.	9.	10.
€12·99 + €10·65 − €7·41	€1·25 + €4·60 − €3·26	€7·42 + €9·60 − €4·95	€3.27 + €9.30 − €7.85	€3·10 + €8·99 − €4·08

11. m cm	12. m cm	13. m cm	14. m cm	15. m cm
1 30 1 10 + 2 60	1 40 3 05 + 1 20	1 30 75 + 2 35	2 36 1 05 + 1 99	2 10 1 49 + 1 70

16.	17.	18.	19.	20.
45 x 7	65 x 9	26 x 9	34 x 5	26 x 7

21.	22.	23.	24.	25.
8)2 9 6	5)7 5 5	6)6 8 4	4)6 0 8	7)4 4 8

Unit 5 - Problems

A Figure it out.

Sam is in 4th class. He has a busy week. Find out about Sam.

1. Sam gets up at 7:30 a.m. Half an hour later he gets the bus at $\boxed{8:00}$.
2. Every school bus journey costs 25c. How much does Sam pay each week? € $\boxed{1.52}$
3. $\frac{1}{3}$ of 4th class are boys. There are 7 boys. How many are girls? $\boxed{}$
4. 4th class pay €2·00 each a week to go swimming. How much is that in total? € $\boxed{}$
5. Children can buy milk at school. $\frac{1}{2}$ the girls buy milk. How many is that? $\boxed{}$
6. On Friday, every 4th class pupil got 2 library books. How many books in total? $\boxed{}$
7. Sam has training for I hr 30 mins. He starts at 10:00 a.m. When does he finish? $\boxed{:}$
8. Tom buys juice for 16c, nuts for 22c and two 5c jellies. How much does he spend? € $\boxed{}$
9. Dad bakes 24 rolls for four children. What equal share do the children get? $\boxed{}$
10. Sam goes to bed 20 minutes before the 9:00 p.m. news. What time is that? $\boxed{:}$ p.m.

$$\begin{array}{r} 25 \\ \times 7 \\ \hline 152 \end{array}$$

B Think it out. Tick (✓) the correct answer.

1. A rectangle is 7 cm wide and 8 cm long. What length is the perimeter?
   a ☐ 15 cm b ☐ 28 cm c ☐ 30 cm

2. 3 boxes weigh 19·5 kg. A weighs 5 kg. B weighs 6·5 kg. What weight is C?
   a ☐ 7 kg b ☐ 7·5 kg c ☐ 8 kg

3. $\frac{1}{6}$ of the 12 crayons in a box are red. How many are red? a ☐ 6 b ☐ 3 c ☐ 2

4. A book has 23 pages. How many pages in 5 books? ☑ 115 b ☐ 105 c ☐ 28

5. Gerry is 154 cm tall. How many metres is that? a ☐ 1·5 m b ☐ 1·54 cm c ☐ 1·54 m

6. 7 boxes of chocolates cost €14·00. How much for 5 boxes?
   a ☐ €10·00 b ☐ €12·00 c ☐ €28·00

7. By how much is 3·42 kg more than I kg?
   a ☐ 1·42 kg b ☐ 1·58 kg c ☐ 2·42 kg

8. A jug had $\frac{1}{4}$ of a litre of milk. How many millilitres was that?
   a ☐ 25 ml b ☐ 250 ml c ☐ 750 ml

9. 65 − 13 + 12 = 80 − 10 ▢
   a ☐ − 4 b ☐ + 6 c ☐ − 6

10. A €12 book was reduced by $\frac{1}{2}$. How much is it now? a ☐ €3 b ☐ €6 c ☐ €9

C Puzzle it out. Do the sums and use the answers to crack the code.

M	528	A	576	N	306	U	726	R	288	S	375	O	952	F	648	E	782

1. 25 x 15 = $\boxed{375}$
2. 56 x 17 =
3. 44 x 12 =
4. 34 x 23 =
5. 75 x 5 =
6. 33 x 22 =
7. 24 x 22 =
8. 125 x 3 =
9. 32 x 18 =
10. 24 x 12 =
11. 46 x 17 =
12. 27 x 24 =
13. 66 x 11 =
14. 51 x 6 =

If you need to, you can work out these sums in your copy.

Sum No.	I	2	3	4	5	6	7	8	9	10	11	12	13	14
Answer	375													
Code	S													

A Tables

1. 3 + **8** = 11   4. 17 − **9** = 8   7. 3 x 8 = **24**   10. 27 ÷ 3 = **7**

2. 6 + 8 = **13**   5. **12** − 3 = 9   8. **7** x 6 = 42

3. **14** − 6 = 7 .   6. [ ] − 9 = 6   9. [ ] ÷ 8 = 4

Score [ ]

B Computation

1.			2.			3.			4.			5.		
	6	9		**2** 0	7		3	4		€8	·2 9			4 8
	3	9	−	3 **5** **3**		x	**3**	9	+	€4	·9 4	x		4
+ 1	8	5		1 5	4		**3 0 6**							
18	**3**								−	€9	·7 8	−	7	9

Give yourself 2 marks for each correct sum.   Score [ ]

C Fractions and Decimals

1. $\frac{1}{4}$ of 80 = [ ]

2. $\frac{1}{3}$ of 9 = [ ]

3. $\frac{1}{6}$ of 12 = [ ]

4. 1·9 + 1·4 = **2.13**

5. 4·5 + 0·5 − 1 = **4.9**

6. 4·5 − 1·5 + 1 = [ ]

7. 1·5 + 2·5 − 1 = [ ]

8. 1·2 + 1·4 + 1·3 = [ ]

9. $\frac{1}{2}$ of 10 less $\frac{1}{4}$ of 8 = [ ]

10. $\frac{1}{2}$ of 12 plus $\frac{1}{4}$ of 4 = [ ]

Score [ ]

D Shapes, Measures and Data... Ring the number that does not belong.

1. $\frac{1}{2}$, (0·25), $\frac{1}{4}$ 3. ($\frac{4}{10}$), 4, 0·4   5. (0·4,) 8 x 5, 4 x 10

2. (0·33,) $\frac{2}{3}$, $\frac{1}{3}$ 4. $\frac{1}{5}$, (0·5), $\frac{1}{2}$

Give yourself 2 marks for each correct answer.   Score [ ]

E Problem Solving... Tick (✓) the correct answer.

1. How many 5c in €1?   a 5   b 10   ✓c 20

2. What is 204c in euros?   ✓ €2·04   b €24   c €2·40

3. By how much is 23 less than 41?   a 14   ✓ 18   c 24

4. What is missing? 21 − 11 ∠ 3 x 5   a >   b =   c <

5. How much for 4 pencils at 31c each?   a 93c   ✓b €1·24   c €1·34

Give yourself 2 marks for each correct answer.   Score [ ]

A Tables

1. 6 x 6 = 36
2. [ ] x 8 = 56
3. 12 x 4 = 48
4. [ ] x 4 = 32
5. 9 x [ ] = 81
6. 5 x [ ] = 40
7. 27 ÷ [ ] = 3
8. [ ] ÷ 10 = 4
9. 50 ÷ [ ] = 5
10. 54 ÷ [ ] = 6
11. [ ] ÷ 7 = 7
12. [ ] ÷ 8 = 8

B Calculate.

1. 14 + 23 + 32 = [ ]
2. 67 − 44 = [ ]
3. (3 x 5) + 20 = [ ]
4. 25 + 40 + 21 = [ ]
5. 120 − [ ] = 100
6. (2 x 11) + 10 = [ ]
7. 42 + 23 + 11 = [ ]
8. 124 ÷ 2 = [ ]
9. 44 + 33 + 22 = [ ]
10. 639 ÷ 3 = [ ]
11. 54 − [ ] = 45
12. [ ] − 13 = 16

C Numbers... Order from smallest to largest.

1. 564, 578, 532   532 , 564 , 578
2. 972, 955, 957   [ ] , [ ] , [ ]
3. 27·9, 29·7, 29·8   [ ] , [ ] , [ ]
4. 36·8, 39·1, 35·9   [ ] , [ ] , [ ]
5. 69·2, 71·1, 71·7   [ ] , [ ] , [ ]
6. 43·5, 42·9, 41·7   [ ] , [ ] , [ ]
7. 1·3, 1·5, 1·4   [ ] , [ ] , [ ]
8. 2·25, 2·5, 2·75   [ ] , [ ] , [ ]
9. 3·4, 4·3, 3·5   [ ] , [ ] , [ ]
10. 1·7, 1·3, 1·5   [ ] , [ ] , [ ]

11. 54 − 2, 56 + 3, 57 − 3   [ ] , [ ] , [ ]
12. 26 + 5, 29 − 3, 28 + 4   [ ] , [ ] , [ ]

D Fractions

1. $\frac{1}{4}$ of 12 = 3
2. $\frac{3}{4}$ of 12 = [ ]
3. $\frac{1}{3}$ of 18 = [ ]
4. $\frac{2}{3}$ of 18 = [ ]
5. $\frac{1}{4}$ of 20 = [ ]
6. $\frac{3}{4}$ of 20 = [ ]
7. $\frac{1}{4}$ of 100 = [ ]
8. $\frac{1}{3}$ of €9·60 = € [ ]
9. $\frac{2}{3}$ of €9·60 = € [ ]
10. $\frac{1}{4}$ of €22·00 = € [ ]
11. $\frac{1}{3}$ of €3·60 = € [ ]
12. ($\frac{1}{3}$ of €3·60) plus €2·00 = € [ ]

E Figure it out. True (✓) or false (✗)?

1. 16 is an even number. [ ]
2. 25 is a multiple of 4. [ ]
3. $\frac{1}{3}$ of 93 is 33. [ ]
4. $\frac{1}{4}$ of 28 is 7. [ ]
5. 15 is one-third of 30. [ ]
6. 9:20 a.m. is night-time. [ ]
7. Squares have only 3 sides. [ ]
8. Three-quarters of 8 is 6. [ ]
9. 1·5 + 0·5 + 0·5 = 2 [ ]
10. 302 > 312 [ ]
11. $\frac{1}{4}$ is greater than $\frac{1}{2}$. [ ]
12. The cost of 6 books at €0·99 is €6·94. [ ]

4/62

A Work it out.

```
1.     4  3        2.   ¹6  2      3.   ²5  5      4.    23  7     5.    46  7
    x  2  7          x      8        x      5        x      4        x      6
    3  0  1          4  9  6         2  7  5         1  4  8        4  0  2

6.   2²2 ²5  6    7.  ¹6 ¹3  3    8.       ¹7  3   9.   ¹4 ¹6  3   10.  ¹1 ¹8  7
       1  7  7           7  8         +     4  5         5  6  7        2  0  8
    +     4  8       + 1  6  8       ¹2  6  6       + 1  2  5       +    7  2
       5  0  1         8  7  9         3  8  4        1 1  5  5        4  6  7

11.   6 2 8 ¹4   12.  4 5 16 5   13. 6 8 5 6 15   14. 5 6 11 2 7  15.  3 4 2 7
     -  1  2  7       -  3  8  3      -     8  9       -  3  5  8      -  2  9  3
      4 5 10 7          1  8  2        0  1 7 6         2 6 9          1  3  4
     +  5  5  5       +  2  1  5      +  4  0  7       +  2  0  9      +  3  4  4
      1  0  6  2        3  9  7        4  8  3          4  7  8        4  7  8

16. ¹1 16 ·2    17.  1 14 ·6   18.   1 14 ·4   19.   4  2 ·5   20.   1  6 ·9
     3  3 ·6          2  0 ·3        1  9 ·9        3  3 ·7         4  2 ·1
   + 2  0 ·4        + 1  1 ·8      + 2  3 ·6      + 1  2 ·2       + 1  0 ·8
     7  0·2           5  5·7         5  5·9         8  8·4         6  9·8
```

B Work it out.

```
1. 6 4 ²2 6     2. 5 9 ⁹8 0    3. 4 6 ⁶2 8    4. 3 4 8 6    5. 5 3 0 5
      7  1           0               0

6. €6 2 ·3 4    7. €1 2 ·4 7   8. €1 ¹4 ⁹9 9  9. €4 7 ⁷5   10. €4 2 ¹1 9
 + €1 9 ·5 5     + €1 3 ·7 7    + €2 5 ·7 3    + €1 1 ·0 9   + €1 2 ·2 9
   7 8 1 8 9  ✗    12 16 ·2 4    39 10 ·7 12    5 8·8 4       5 4 14·4 8
 - €2 5 ·3 8     - €1 9 ·1 8    - €1 5 ·6 8    - €3 1 ·8 4   - €1 6 ·3 5
   5 6 ·5 1        0 5·0 6        2 5·0 4        2 7 0 0       3 8·1 3

11.   m  cm     12.   m  cm     13.   m  cm    14.   m  cm    15.   m  cm
     1  2  9          1 14  0         2 1 9 0       1 2 4 9        3 16  3
     2  4  6              8  5        2 8  5        3 4  5         2  6  5
   + 1  8  7        + 4  6  6       +    7  0     + 1 8  8       + 1  0  4
     5  6  2          6  9  1         5  4  5       7  5  2        7  3  2

16.   1 3  2    17.    2  3    18.   5 6  7    19.   4 1  9    20.  3 6  4
    x      7        x      5        x      8        x      5        x      8
    2  2  4         1  1  5         5  3  6         9  5           5  1  2
```

25

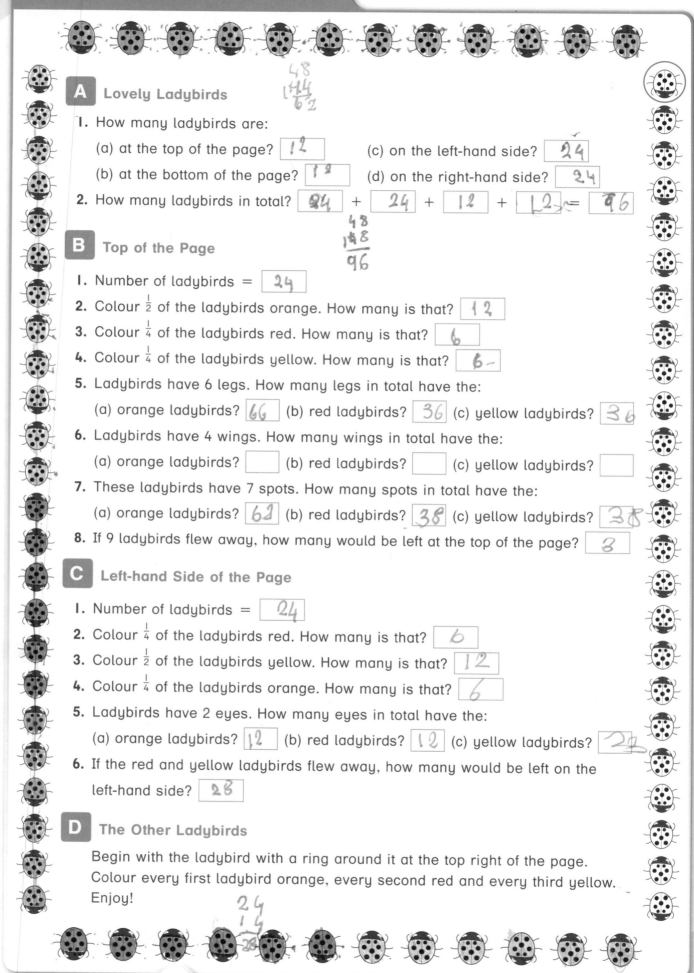

Unit 6 – Problems

A Lovely Ladybirds

48
144
6 2

1. How many ladybirds are:

   (a) at the top of the page? `12`   (c) on the left-hand side? `24`

   (b) at the bottom of the page? `12`   (d) on the right-hand side? `24`

2. How many ladybirds in total? `24` + `24` + `12` + `12` = `96`

48
148
96

B Top of the Page

1. Number of ladybirds = `24`

2. Colour $\frac{1}{2}$ of the ladybirds orange. How many is that? `12`

3. Colour $\frac{1}{4}$ of the ladybirds red. How many is that? `6`

4. Colour $\frac{1}{4}$ of the ladybirds yellow. How many is that? `6`

5. Ladybirds have 6 legs. How many legs in total have the:

   (a) orange ladybirds? `66` (b) red ladybirds? `36` (c) yellow ladybirds? `36`

6. Ladybirds have 4 wings. How many wings in total have the:

   (a) orange ladybirds? [ ] (b) red ladybirds? [ ] (c) yellow ladybirds? [ ]

7. These ladybirds have 7 spots. How many spots in total have the:

   (a) orange ladybirds? `62` (b) red ladybirds? `38` (c) yellow ladybirds? `38`

8. If 9 ladybirds flew away, how many would be left at the top of the page? `3`

C Left-hand Side of the Page

1. Number of ladybirds = `24`

2. Colour $\frac{1}{4}$ of the ladybirds red. How many is that? `6`

3. Colour $\frac{1}{2}$ of the ladybirds yellow. How many is that? `12`

4. Colour $\frac{1}{4}$ of the ladybirds orange. How many is that? `6`

5. Ladybirds have 2 eyes. How many eyes in total have the:

   (a) orange ladybirds? `12` (b) red ladybirds? `12` (c) yellow ladybirds? `24`

6. If the red and yellow ladybirds flew away, how many would be left on the left-hand side? `28`

D The Other Ladybirds

Begin with the ladybird with a ring around it at the top right of the page. Colour every first ladybird orange, every second red and every third yellow. Enjoy!

24
14
28

★ Score each exercise out of 10.

A Tables

1. 5 + 12 = [ ]
2. 9 + 11 = [ ]
3. 5 + [ ] = 16
4. 14 − 5 = [ ]
5. 20 − [ ] = 10
6. [ ] − 9 = 7
7. 5 × 7 = [ ]
8. [ ] × 9 = 45
9. [ ] ÷ 8 = 6
10. 35 ÷ [ ] = 5

Score [ ]

B Computation

1.			1		8
		2	0		
	+		5	5	
		9	8	7	

2.	3	9	6
×		7	

3.	m	cm
	4	1	8
	5	8	6
+	5	2	4

4.	€7	·0	9
−	€6	·4	0
×			4

5.		4	5	6
	+	3	9	9
	−	6	2	8

Give yourself 2 marks for each correct sum. Score [ ]

C Fractions and Decimals... Choose a correct answer from the list for each question.

0·9   0·7   3·5   0·5   1   2·5   4   1·5   0·1   0·3

1. $\frac{3}{10}$ = [ ]
2. 2 + 2 − 0·5 = [ ]
3. $\frac{1}{2}$ = [ ]
4. 1 + 0·5 + 1 = [ ]
5. $\frac{7}{10}$ = [ ]
6. 4 − 2·5 = [ ]
7. $\frac{1}{10}$ = [ ]
8. $\frac{3}{10} + \frac{7}{10}$ = [ ]
9. $\frac{9}{10}$ = [ ]
10. 1·5 + 2·5 = [ ]

Score [ ]

D Shapes, Measures and Data... Write **height**, **weight**, **length**, **capacity** or **width**.

1. _____
2. _____
3. _____
4. _____
5. _____

Give yourself 2 marks for each correct answer. Score [ ]

E Problem Solving

Mum made 30 buns. She put pink icing on 6. She put green icing on half of the rest. She put orange icing on a quarter of the remaining buns. Tom took half of all the buns to school for a cake sale. He sold the buns for 10c each.

1. How many buns were not pink? [ ]
2. How many buns were green? [ ]
3. How many buns were orange? [ ]
4. How many buns did Tom take to school? [ ]
5. How much in total did Tom get for the buns? € [ ]

Give yourself 2 marks for each correct answer. Score [ ]

Unit 7 - Quick Questions

A Tables

1. 10 + ☐ = 19
2. 9 + ☐ = 15
3. 13 − ☐ = 8
4. ☐ − 8 = 9
5. ☐ + 9 = 17
6. 2 x ☐ = 14
7. ☐ x 6 = 36
8. 4 x ☐ = 36
9. 24 ÷ ☐ = 3
10. 27 ÷ ☐ = 9
11. ☐ ÷ 5 = 11
12. ☐ ÷ 4 = 6

B Calculate.

1. 14 + ☐ = 16
2. 17 + ☐ = 39
3. ☐ + 24 = 47
4. 76 − ☐ = 32
5. 45 − ☐ = 22
6. 46 − ☐ = 15
7. (5 x 5) + 9 = ☐
8. (3 x 11) + 4 = ☐
9. (2 x 12) + 5 = ☐
10. (3 x 10) − 6 = ☐
11. (36 ÷ 6) + 4 = ☐
12. (49 ÷ 7) + 1 = ☐

C Numbers... Complete the tables.

Tables	7	9	11	13	15	17	19	21	23	25
− 2			9							23
+ 5	12							26		
− 7		2				10				
+ 9					24				32	

D Money... How much change from €2·00?

1. Spent 43c and €1·20. ☐ c left.
2. Spent 19c and €1·50. ☐ c left.
3. Spent 68c and 40c. ☐ c left.
4. Spent 59c and €1·10. ☐ c left.
5. Spent 24c and €1·25. ☐ c left.
6. Spent 40c and €1·35. ☐ c left.
7. Spent 99c and 50c. ☐ c left.
8. Spent 17c and 90c. ☐ c left.
9. Spent 82c and 20c. ☐ c left.
10. Spent 70c and 35c. ☐ c left.
11. Spent 35c and €1·45. ☐ c left.
12. Spent 73c and €1·00. ☐ c left.

E Figure it out. Tick (✓) the correct answer.

1. (66 ÷ 3) + 10 = a 21 b 32 c 43
2. (12 x 2) − 8 = a 16 b 20 c 24
3. (5 x 5) − 4 = a 19 b 21 c 23
4. (28 ÷ 4) + 2 = a 7 b 8 c 9
5. (3 x 9) − 4 = a 21 b 23 c 25
6. $\frac{1}{8}$ of 88 = a 8 b 9 c 11
7. $\frac{1}{7}$ of 56 = a 7 b 8 c 9
8. 0·25 of 48 = a 12 b 23 c 24
9. (€1·20 + €1·30) x 4 =
   a €5·00 b €7·50 c €10·00
10. 2 m 30 cm =
    a 23 cm b 203 cm c 230 cm
11. €2·20 + €1·49 + €1·10 =
    a €3·79 b €3·99 c €4·79
12. 2 m 50 cm + 1 m 99 cm =
    a 4 m 29 cm b 4 m 49 cm c 4 m 99 cm

A Work it out.

1.		4	5		2.		6	2		3.		5	4		4.		7	8		5.		6	7
	x		4			x		6			x		7			x		5			x		5

| 6. | 4 | 5 | 6 | 4 | 7. | 7 | 2 | 2 | 4 | 8. | 5 | 6 | 4 | 5 | 9. | 4 | 2 | 8 | 8 | 10. | 6 | 5 | 0 | 4 |

11.	7	6	7	4	12.	5	3	8	9	13.	6	9	0	9	14.	8	2	8	8	15.	4	7	4	2
			R					R					R										R	

16.		5	6		17.		7	3		18.		4	8		19.		2	7		20.		8	5
	x		9			x		4			x		7			x		6			x		9

B Work it out.

1.		8	4		2.		5	7		3.		5	2		4.	4	6	5	3	5.	2	6	5	7
	x		5			x		7			x		9		−	2	9	8	7	−	2	3	3	8

6.		3	0	4	7.			7	1	8.		4	8	7	9.		3	6	7	10.		5	2	8
		2	0	4			3	6	5			3	0	6			2	7	7			2	5	7
	+	3	8	6		+	2	6	5		+	5	0	1		+	2	1	9		+	1	5	6

11.		6	7		12.		7	3		13.		3	8		14.		7	9		15.		5	6
	x		9			x		6			x		9			x		4			x		8

16.	€1	·7	0	17.		€6	·3	3	18.		€9	·2	6	19.		€8	·2	0	20.		€6	·0	9
+	€8	·4	7		+	€8	·0	5		+	€7	·4	3		+	€4	·6	6		+	€3	·1	7
−	€7	·6	9		−	€4	·2	0		−	€8	·0	9		−	€5	·9	8		−	€2	·4	5

21.		5	2	9	22.		4	7	6	23.		6	1	3	24.	4	6	5	3	25.	2	6	5	7
	−	2	7	8		−	1	8	9		−	3	1	7	−	2	9	8	7	−	2	3	3	8

Unit 7 – Problems

A   Figure it out.

1. What time is 20 mins after 2:15 p.m.? ☐ p.m.

2. Seán gets €2·50 pocket money. Ann gets twice as much. How much does Ann get? € ☐

3. Colm and Cora bought a pizza for €4·60. How much did each pay? € ☐

4. Oranges are 20c each or 3 for 50c. How much for 8 oranges? € ☐

5. There are 4 cows and 6 ducks on a farm. How many legs are there altogether? ☐

6. Seán pays 30c bus fare a day from Monday to Friday. How much is that each week? € ☐

7. Molly had €14·50 in her purse. How much was left after spending €2·20 and €1·30? € ☐

8. Half of the 28 children in fourth class have blue eyes. How many is that? ☐

9. John had 15 toy cars. He sold $\frac{1}{3}$ of them to Pat at €1·00 each. How much did Pat pay? € ☐

10. 7 kiwis + 4 bananas + 8 apples + 2 pears = ☐ pieces of fruit

B   Think it out. Tick (✓) the correct answer.

1. Five thousand, seven hundred and seventy-five = ☐a 5705 ☐b 5775 ☐c 5757

2. Three packets of 6 apples at €2·50 a packet cost ☐a €6·00 ☐b €7·50 ☐c €15·00

3. How much for 8 litres of petrol at €1·50 a litre? ☐a €9·50 ☐b €12·00 ☐c €16·00

4. A bus left at 8:35 a.m. and travelled for 45 mins. It arrived at ☐a 8:45 a.m. ☐b 9:10 a.m. ☐c 9:20 a.m.

5. How many 7s in 37? ☐a 5 ☐b 6 ☐c 7

6. How many sides have 3 triangles? ☐a 3 ☐b 9 ☐c 12

7. By how much is 166 less than 269? ☐a 103 ☐b 133 ☐c 139

8. What is $\frac{1}{2}$ of 18 plus $\frac{1}{4}$ of 16? ☐a 6 ☐b 13 ☐c 10

9. What is missing? 50 – 14 ☐ 6 x 6 ☐a > ☐b = ☐c <

10. A farmer's cows have a total of 48 legs. How many cows has he? ☐a 8 ☐b 12 ☐c 24

C   Puzzle it out. Use the 100-square to complete the tasks.

> A **multiple** is a number that can be divided by another number without leaving a remainder. 5 is a multiple of 5.

1. Ring every 6th number, starting with number 6.

2. Write 5 multiples of 9. 18, ☐, ☐, ☐, ☐

3. What number is 27 less than 92? ☐

4. Put a line through every 7th number, starting with 14.

5. Write 5 multiples of 7. 14, ☐, ☐, ☐, ☐

6. Start at 81 and count back 32 to ☐.

7. Put an x on any number that is a multiple of 8.

8. Write every 6th number from 72 backwards.
   72, ☐, ☐, ☐, ☐, ☐, ☐, ☐, ☐

9. Write four numbers that divide evenly into 12.
   ☐, ☐, ☐, ☐

10. Write four numbers that divide evenly into 20. ☐, ☐, ☐, ☐

1	2	3	4	5	⑥	7	8̸	9	10
11	12	13	1̸4̸	15	16	17	18	19	20
21	22	23	24	25	26	27	28	29	30
31	32	33	34	35	36	37	38	39	40
41	42	43	44	45	46	47	48	49	50
51	52	53	54	55	56	57	58	59	60
61	62	63	64	65	66	67	68	69	70
71	72	73	74	75	76	77	78	79	80
81	82	83	84	85	86	87	88	89	90
91	92	93	94	95	96	97	98	99	100

Unit 7 - Check-up

A Tables

1. $4 +$ ____ $= 9$
2. $7 + 9 =$ ____
3. $9 +$ ____ $= 18$

4. ____ $- 9 = 7$
5. $13 - 7 =$ ____
6. ____ $- 4 = 9$

7. $9 \times$ ____ $= 72$
8. $35 \div$ ____ $= 5$
9. ____ $\times 8 = 56$

10. ____ $\div 9 = 9$

Score ____

B Computation

1.		5	0	2.		7	3	3.			3	4.	€9	·2	8	5.		4	9
	−	4	2		×		6			7			€8	·0	7		+	8	5
		8	6						+	9	4		+ €6	·5	2				
									1	8	6						−	7	8

Give yourself 2 marks for each correct sum.

Score ____

C Fractions and Decimals... Tick (✓) the correct answer.

1. $4·6 - 2·5 =$ a 2·1   b 6·1   c 7·3
2. $2·7 + 0·8 =$ a 2·1   b 3·5   c 10·7
3. $0·1$ of $50 =$ a 5   b 10   c 25
4. $0·5$ of $24 =$ a 6   b 9   c 12
5. $\frac{1}{6}$ of $12 =$ a 2   b 3   c 6

6. $1·3 + 1·3 - 1 =$ a 1·3   b 1·6   c 2·6
7. $2·5 + 4 - 1·5 =$ a 3   b 4   c 5
8. $4·5 - 1·5 - 1 =$ a 2   b 2·5   c 3
9. $5·1 + 1·9 + 1 =$ a 6·2   b 7·1   c 8
10. $\frac{1}{4}$ of $12·4 =$ a 3·1   b 4·1   c 6·2

Score ____

D Shapes, Measures and Data

307 405163

1. How many €1·25 raffle tickets can I buy with €5·00? ____
2. If the tickets are 2 for €2·00, how many €1·25 tickets will I get if I spend €5·25? ____
3. Which measure is greater: metre or kilometre? ____
4. Which measure is greater: litre or millilitre? ____
5. Which measure is greater: gram or kilogram? ____

Give yourself 2 marks for each correct answer.

Score ____

E Problem Solving

1. 20 people on a boat trip paid €1·50 each. How much in total did they pay? € ____
2. Jim ran three 250 m laps on sports day. How much altogether did he run? ____ m
3. One-third of the 24 children in 4th class have brown eyes. How many is that? ____
4. A coat cost €40. Mary got €5·40 off in the sale. How much did Mary pay? € ____
5. Zoo tickets cost €2 for adults and €1·50 for children. How much for 2 adults and 3 children? € ____

Give yourself 2 marks for each correct answer.

Score ____

Unit 8 - Quick Questions

A Tables

1. ☐ x 3 = 18
4. ☐ x 8 = 56
7. 42 ÷ ☐ = 6
10. 32 ÷ ☐ = 4

2. 6 x ☐ = 48
5. ☐ x 2 = 16
8. ☐ ÷ 6 = 8
11. ☐ ÷ 9 = 9

3. 7 x ☐ = 49
6. 5 x ☐ = 45
9. 54 ÷ ☐ = 9
12. ☐ ÷ 4 = 7

B Calculate.

1. (4 x 6) + 6 = ☐
5. 167 − ☐ = 123
9. 69 ÷ 3 = ☐

2. (8 x 3) − 2 = ☐
6. 264 − ☐ = 223
10. 84 ÷ 4 = ☐

3. (9 x 3) − 6 = ☐
7. (5 x 7) + ☐ = 39
11. (25 ÷ 5) + ☐ = 7

4. (7 x 11) + 5 = ☐
8. 4 x 2 x 5 = ☐
12. (36 ÷ 6) + ☐ = 9

C Numbers... Complete the sequences.

1. 57, 47, 37, ☐, ☐, ☐
7. 12, 24, 36, ☐, ☐, ☐

2. 6, 13, 20, ☐, ☐, ☐
8. 63, 56, 49, ☐, ☐, ☐

3. 81, 72, 63, ☐, ☐, ☐
9. 6·5, 6, 5·5, ☐, ☐, ☐

4. 7, 14, 21, ☐, ☐, ☐
10. 6·5, 8·5, 10·5, ☐, ☐, ☐

5. 46, 49, 52, ☐, ☐, ☐
11. 5c, 10c, 15c, ☐, ☐, ☐

6. 26, 30, 34, ☐, ☐, ☐
12. 50c, 75c, €1·00, ☐, ☐, ☐

D Money... Find the cost of each shopping list.

 Sandwich (S) = 80c   Fruit (F) = 20c   Yoghurt (Y) = 35c

1. 1S + 1F + 1Y = €**1.35c**
7. 1S + 2F + 1Y = €☐

2. 2Y + 2F = €**1,10c**
8. 2S + 1F + 1Y = €☐

3. 1S + 3F + 1Y = €☐
9. 1S + 5F = €☐

4. 2S + 2F = €☐
10. 2S + 4F = €☐

5. 1S + 4F + 2Y = €☐
11. 4S + 1F + 2Y = €☐

6. 2S + 2F + 2Y = €€☐
12. 5S + 5F = €☐

E Figure it out. Use +, −, x or ÷ to complete the number sentences.

1. (2 ☐ 7) ☐ 10 = 90
7. 2 ☐ 3 ☐ 4 = 24

2. (3 ☐ 3) ☐ 3 = 18
8. (10 ☐ 2) ☐ $3\frac{1}{2}$ = $16\frac{1}{2}$

3. 10 ☐ 4 ☐ 2 = 4
9. (5 ☐ 7) ☐ 15 = 20

4. (8 ☐ 2) ☐ 4 = 20
10. (7 ☐ 3) ☐ 10 = 31

5. (€2·30 ☐ 2) ☐ €0·40 = €5·00
11. (4 ☐ 2) ☐ 2 = 10

6. (€4·50 ☐ 2) ☐ €1·00 = €8·00
12. (24 ☐ 2) ☐ 2 = 6

A Work it out.

1.
```
    7 6
  x   4
```

2.
```
    3 8
  x   5
```

3.
```
    5 8
  x   9
```

4.
```
    4 8
  x   3
```

5.
```
    4 2
  x   8
```

6.
```
    2 3 4
    3 4 3
  + 7 1 4
```

7.
```
    5 2 6
      7 5
  +   8 6
```

8.
```
  3 4 7 2
  1 6 1 8
+ 2 6 6 7
```

9.
```
  3 6 5 5
  1 7 5 4
+ 1 9 2 2
```

10.
```
  2 0 3 5
  1 6 1 6
+   1 9 8
```

11.
```
  5 1 1 2
- 3 2 8 9
```

12.
```
  1 8 7 7
- 1 6 5 8
```

13.
```
  3 7 6 6
- 1 5 3 7
```

14.
```
  3 0 7 4
- 1 3 6 7
```

15.
```
  6 2 6 2
- 4 1 8 4
```

16. 4)264
17. 8)168
18. 7)379 R
19. 6)412 R
20. 9)306

B Work it out.

1.
```
  4 8 8 3
- 2 0 6 6
```

2.
```
  1 8 6 9
-   7 8 0
```

3.
```
  3 0 1 0
- 1 4 2 6
```

4.
```
  4 1 5 5
- 2 9 9 9
```

5.
```
  3 0 4 5
- 1 6 7 0
```

6.
```
    2 0 8
  + 6 7 5
  - 3 7 7
```

7.
```
    4 1 9
  + 3 8 8
  - 1 7 8
```

8.
```
    2 6 4
  + 1 9 9
  - 1 8 4
```

9.
```
    5 2 7
  + 3 6 6
  - 2 8 9
```

10.
```
    1 6 3
  + 4 2 0
  - 2 5 7
```

11.
```
  €2 ·8 8
  x     3
```

12.
```
  €3 ·0 9
  x     6
```

13.
```
  €8 ·1 5
  x     5
```

14.
```
  €6 ·2 7
  x     4
```

15.
```
  €5 ·0 9
  x     7
```

16.
```
    4 8
  x   7
```

17.
```
    5 9
  x   6
```

18.
```
    8 7
  x   6
```

19.
```
    2 8
  x   9
```

20.
```
    3 7
  x   8
```

21.
```
  €4 0 ·5 2
  €3 4 ·1 9
+ €1 7 ·3 3
```

22.
```
  €3 0 ·0 2
  €2 1 ·1 8
+ €3 0 ·1 4
```

23.
```
  €1 4 ·3 2
  €2 0 ·1 2
+ €3 5 ·4 0
```

24.
```
  €1 7 ·0 7
  €2 5 ·6 0
+ €3 9 ·0 7
```

25.
```
  €3 8 ·4 5
  €2 2 ·4 5
+ €1 3 ·0 7
```

A   Figure it out.

Toby had a box of 36 marbles. Jed, Molly and Pat were playing with Toby.

1. $\frac{1}{4}$ of the marbles were green. How many were green? ☐

2. $\frac{1}{6}$ of the marbles were red. How many were red? ☐

3. $\frac{1}{3}$ of the marbles were yellow. How many were yellow? ☐

4. How many marbles were not green, red or yellow? ☐

5. There was only 1 pink marble and the rest were blue or orange.

   How many were blue or orange? ☐

B   Think it out. Tick (✓) the correct answer.

1. How many €3·30 train tickets can you buy for €19·80? a 5 b 6 b 7

2. Break is from 10:35 a.m. to 10:50 a.m. How long is that? a 15 mins b 25 mins c 35 mins

3. How many 8s in 74? a 9 b 8 b 7

4. By how much is 21·5 greater than 18·3? a 3·8 b 3·2 c 2·8

5. What is missing? 9 x 8 ▨ 7 x 12 a > b = c <

C   Puzzle it out. Do the sums and complete the cross-number puzzle.

Across

1.		2	4	5	3.		6	8	7	6.		4	9	3	8.		6	5	4	9.			9
	+	5	0	1		−	2	9	9		−		7	7		−	2	3	3			x	3

10.			9	11.		2	5	13.	3	9	2	5	15.	1	0	7	0	16.		1	3	0
	x	9			x		5	+	1	6	2	7	+		3	2	0		x			5

Down

2.		8	0	1	3.			7	4.	4	3	2	1	5.	6	7	9	9	7.		1	2
	−	1	9	9		x		5	+	4	1	2	3	−	2	6	7	8		x	1	0

12.		7	6	8	14.		1	1	9
	−	1	9	9		+	4	6	6

A Tables

1. $8 + 6 =$ ☐

2. $9 -$ ☐ $= 8$

3. ☐ $- 6 = 9$

4. ☐ $- 10 = 8$

5. ☐ $- 3 = 9$

6. ☐ $- 9 = 7$

7. $6 \times 8 =$ ☐

8. ☐ $\times 8 = 56$

9. ☐ $\div 9 = 6$

10. ☐ $\div 8 = 5$

Score ☐

B Computation

1.		3	8
	1	0	7
+		6	9

2.		4	0
−		9	9
	1	0	9

3.		7	8
×			5

4.	€9	·9	6
+ €7	·0	4	
− €8	·0	0	

5.		6	9
	×		6
−	1	5	4

Give yourself 2 marks for each correct sum.

Score ☐

C Fractions and Decimals

1. $\frac{1}{10}$ of $60 =$ ☐

2. $\frac{1}{3}$ of $33 =$ ☐

3. $\frac{1}{5}$ of $15 =$ ☐

4. $4{\cdot}2 - 0{\cdot}8 =$ ☐

5. $4{\cdot}5 - 1{\cdot}2 + 0{\cdot}8 =$ ☐

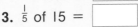
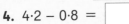

6. $2{\cdot}3 + 1{\cdot}3 + 1{\cdot}2 =$ ☐

7. $5 - 1{\cdot}5 - 1 =$ ☐

8. $1{\cdot}7 + 1{\cdot}4 + 1{\cdot}1 =$ ☐

9. $\frac{1}{4}$ of 16 less $\frac{1}{3}$ of $9 =$ ☐

10. $\frac{1}{2}$ of 12 plus $\frac{1}{3}$ of $6 =$ ☐

Score ☐

D Shapes, Measures and Data

What am I?

1. I am a small measure, about the size of your nail. I measure length.

   ☐

2. I have four sides. Two opposite sides are 3 cm and the other sides are 5 cm.

   ☐

Answer the questions.

3. I have 250 ml written on my packet. Am I sugar, juice or string? ☐

4. How much change will I have from €10·00 if I spend €3·49 and €2·50? € ☐

5. How much change will I have from €10·00 if I spend €4·50 and €1·45? € ☐

Give yourself 2 marks for each correct answer.

Score ☐

E Problem Solving… Tick (✓) the correct answer.

1. How many 12s in 80? | a 6 | b 7 | c 8 |

2. How many one-fifths in 1 whole number? | a 1 | b 3 | c 5 |

3. By how much is 23·5 less than 28·2? | a 4·3 | b 4·7 | c 5·3 |

4. What is missing? $3{\cdot}1 - 1{\cdot}2$ ▨ $5 - 3$ | a > | b = | c < |

5. How much for 7 bars at 41c each? | a €2·87 | b €2·14 | c €4·17 |

Give yourself 2 marks for each correct answer.

Score ☐

A Tables

1. 7 + ☐ = 16   4. 18 – 9 = ☐   7. 9 x 6 = ☐   10. 63 ÷ ☐ = 9

2. 10 + ☐ = 17   5. 7 + 9 = ☐   8. 6 x ☐ = 54   11. 81 ÷ 9 = ☐

3. 14 – ☐ = 10   6. 6 x ☐ = 48   9. 27 ÷ ☐ = 3   12. 36 ÷ ☐ = 4

B Calculate.

1. 129 + 111 = ☐   5. 174 – 129 = ☐   9. 67 + 22 + 111 = ☐

2. 345 – 47 = ☐   6. 12 x 6 = ☐   10. 24 + 27 + 33 = ☐

3. 499 + 24 = ☐   7. 606 ÷ 3 = ☐   11. 155 – ☐ = 120

4. 38 + 454 = ☐   8. 149 + 113 + 30 = ☐   12. ☐ – 13 = 123

C Numbers… Are these numbers > (greater than) or < (less than) or = (equal to) each other?

1. 98 ☐ 89   7. 42 + 8 + 20 ☐ 90

2. 45 + 10 ☐ 54 – 6   8. 15 x 10 ☐ 100 + 30

3. 537 + 100 ☐ 565 – 100   9. 1·5 + 2·5 ☐ 3

4. 879 – 20 ☐ 897 – 10   10. 0·25 + 0·25 ☐ 0·5

5. 31 x 4 ☐ 100   11. 5 – 1 ☐ 1·5 + 2·5

6. 12 x 9 ☐ 8 x 12   12. 2 – 1·5 ☐ 1 + 0·5

D Money… Write as euros and cents.

1. 496c €☐   5. 660c €☐   9. 905c €☐

2. 655c €☐   6. 487c €☐   10. 45c €☐

3. 982c €☐   7. 876c €☐   11. 327c €☐

4. 776c €☐   8. 240c €☐   12. 540c €☐

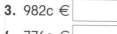

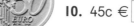

E Figure it out. True (✓) or false (✗)?

1. 17 is divisible by 6. ☐

2. 54 is a multiple of 9. ☐

3. $\frac{1}{3}$ of 66 is 33. ☐

4. $\frac{1}{4}$ of 84 is 24. ☐

5. €1·25 is one-third of €3·75. ☐

6. There are 15 minutes in a quarter of an hour. ☐

7. A sphere has corners. ☐

8. 1·25 is greater than 1·5. ☐

9. 3·25 + 1 + 2·25 = 6·5 ☐

10. 625 – 120 < 677 ☐

11. One-third of 18 is 6. ☐

12. €1·25 – €0·99 = €0·26 ☐

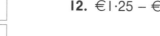

A — Work it out.

1.
```
   4 8
 x   9
```

2.
```
   6 7
 x   9
```

3.
```
   4 7
 x   8
```

4.
```
   3 5
 x   8
```

5.
```
 x
```

6.
```
   3 8 2
   1 1 8
 +   7 7
```

7.
```
   2 3 6
   3 4 7
 + 2 5 6
```

8.
```
   1 8 4
   1 2 9
 + 7 0 8
```

9.
```
   4 1 6
   3 5 7
 +   2 9
```

10.
```
   1 3 7
   4 9 9
 + 1 9 3
```

11.
```
   2 3 4
   3 4 3
 + 7 1 4
```

12.
```
 3 6 5 5
 2 7 4 4
 + 1 9 2 2
```

13.
```
 1 4 7 2
 4 6 6 7
 + 2 6 1 8
```

14.
```
 3 6 5 5
 4 0 7 4
 +   6 1 8
```

15.
```
 1 3 2 4
 4 0 0 6
 + 1 9 2 5
```

16.
```
   3 6
   1 4
 + 1 6
   6 6
```

17.
```
   4
   5
 + 2 2
   8 0
```

18.
```
   3
   6
 + 3 3
   9 5
```

19.
```
   1
   4
 + 2 6
   5 8
```

20.
```
   4
   5
 + 2 4
   9 9
```

B — Work it out.

1.
```
   5 1 1 2
 - 3 2 8 9
```

2.
```
   1 8 7 7
 - 1 6 5 8
```

3.
```
   2 7 6 6
 - 1 5 3 7
```

4.
```
   6 2 6 2
 - 4 1 8 4
```

5.
```
   5 4 6 1
 - 2 0 0 9
```

6.
```
   5 6 2
 + 1 8 5

 - 4 2 0
```

7.
```
   3 6 2
 + 4 7 7

 - 2 0 4
```

8.
```
   5 1 7
 + 1 2 8

 - 2 7 9
```

9.
```
   4 8 6
 +   6 6

 - 1 8 7
```

10.
```
   4 3 4
 +   9 6

 - 2 6 6
```

11.
```
   € 4 · 0 6
   €1 9 · 5 4
 + €3 6 · 2 0
```

12.
```
   €3 3 · 1 4
   €1 6 · 5 2
 + €2 3 · 0 5
```

13.
```
   € 9 · 2 1
   €5 1 · 1 5
 + €2 9 · 4 7
```

14.
```
   €1 4 · 6 8
   €2 6 · 5 3
 + €3 7 · 2 2
```

15.
```
   €3 7 · 1 2
   €1 8 · 9 7
 + €2 0 · 0 4
```

16.
```
   4 6
 x   9
```

17.
```
   6 3
 x   7
```

18.
```
   9 4
 x   8
```

19.
```
   1 7
 x   7
```

20.
```
   4 6
 x   7
```

21.
```
   4 0
 x   7
```

22.
```
   7 2
 x   8
```

23.
```
   6 6
 x   3
```

24.
```
   4 7
 x   5
```

25.
```
   5 3
 x   6
```

A Making Shapes: Animal Antics... Draw these animals using only the shapes below. Colour the pictures.

1. Duck

2. Dog

3. Cat

4. Crocodile

5. Penguin

6. Giraffe

Unit 9 - Check-up

A Tables

1. 20 – ☐ = 10   4. 14 – ☐ = 5   7. 4 x 12 = ☐   10. 45 ÷ ☐ = 5

2. ☐ x 9 = 27   5. 17 – ☐ = 9   8. ☐ x 10 = 80

3. 5 + ☐ = 15   6. ☐ – 6 = 4   9. 63 ÷ 7 = ☐

Score ☐

B Computation

1.			4	2	2.	3	8	4	3.		m	cm	4.	€1	0	·5	5	5.		7	2	6
			1	9							1	08	–	€9	·6	7				5	0	8
	+		5	5	x			4			4	66						+	1	6	3
		9	2	0					+		3	50	x				5				

Give yourself 2 marks for each correct sum.

Score ☐

C Fractions and Decimals... Ring the correct amount.

1.	$\frac{5}{6}$	♥ ♥ ♥ ♥ ♥ ♥ ♥ ♥ ♥ ♥ ♥ ♥	6.	$\frac{2}{3}$	🚲 🚲 🚲 🚲 🚲 🚲
2.	0·7	🎗 🎗 🎗 🎗 🎗 🎗 🎗 🎗 🎗 🎗	7.	$\frac{2}{5}$	☺ ☺ ☺ ☺ ☺ ☺ ☺ ☺ ☺ ☺
3.	$\frac{1}{6}$	🚓 🚓 🚓 🚓 🚓 🚓 🚓 🚓 🚓 🚓	8.	0·4	🏠 🏠 🏠 🏠 🏠 🏠 🏠 🏠 🏠 🏠
4.	0·5	🚩 🚩 🚩 🚩 🚩 🚩 🚩 🚩	9.	$\frac{1}{2}$	🚚 🚚 🚚 🚚 🚚 🚚 🚚 🚚 🚚 🚚
5.	$\frac{3}{4}$	👂 👂 👂 👂 👂 👂 👂 👂 👂 👂	10.	$\frac{5}{8}$	✦ ✦ ✦ ✦ ✦ ✦ ✦ ✦

Score ☐

D Shapes, Measures and Data... Write **capacity**, **distance**, **length**, **time** or **weight**.

1. _____   2. _____   3. _____   4. _____   5. _____

Give yourself 2 marks for each correct answer.

Score ☐

E Problem Solving

A fisherman caught 48 fish. He sold one-quarter of the fish to his brother for 50c each. He brought home $\frac{1}{8}$ of the total catch. One-sixth of all the fish were mackerel. He cooked half of the fish he brought home for dinner.

1. How many fish did he sell to his brother? ☐

2. How many fish did he bring home? ☐

3. How many fish were mackerel? ☐

4. How many fish did he cook for dinner? ☐

5. How much money did he get from his brother? € ☐

Give yourself 2 marks for each correct answer.

Score ☐

Unit 10 - Quick Questions

A Tables

1. $4 \times \boxed{} = 32$
2. $\boxed{} \times 9 = 36$
3. $8 \times \boxed{} = 64$
4. $\boxed{} \times 9 = 54$
5. $7 \times \boxed{} = 49$
6. $9 \times \boxed{} = 45$
7. $45 \div \boxed{} = 5$
8. $\boxed{} \div 6 = 5$
9. $54 \div \boxed{} = 9$
10. $\boxed{} \div 5 = 7$
11. $\boxed{} \div 3 = 8$
12. $36 \div \boxed{} = 9$

B Calculate.

1. $42 + 13 + 12 = \boxed{}$
2. $54 - 22 = \boxed{}$
3. $123 + 132 = \boxed{}$
4. $17 + \boxed{} = 50$
5. $96 - 43 = \boxed{}$
6. $(11 \times 7) + 3 = \boxed{}$
7. $396 \div 3 = \boxed{}$
8. $(16 \div 4) - 1 = \boxed{}$
9. $0\cdot5 + 4\cdot5 = \boxed{}$
10. $€6\cdot41 - €2\cdot20 = €\boxed{}$
11. $1 - 0\cdot5 + 2 = \boxed{}$
12. $\boxed{} - 13 = 12$

C Numbers... Are these numbers $>$ (greater than), $<$ (less than) or $=$ (equal to) each other?

1. $90 \div 3 \ \boxed{} \ 32$
2. $66 + 33 \ \boxed{} \ 100$
3. $912 - 100 \ \boxed{} \ 722 + 100$
4. $513 \div 3 \ \boxed{} \ 422 + 50$
5. $51 \times 4 \ \boxed{} \ 204$
6. $15 \times 6 \ \boxed{} \ 8 \times 12$
7. $33 + 6 + 11 \ \boxed{} \ 22 + 12 + 12$
8. $20 \times 10 \ \boxed{} \ 100 + 100$
9. $1\cdot4 + 2\cdot2 + 1\cdot3 \ \boxed{} \ 8$
10. $0\cdot25 + 0\cdot25 + 0\cdot25 \ \boxed{} \ 0\cdot75$
11. $€2\cdot30 + €3\cdot40 \ \boxed{} \ €5\cdot00$
12. $€4\cdot10 + €1\cdot50 \ \boxed{} \ €5\cdot60$

D Fractions

1. one-half of 6 = $\boxed{}$
2. one-quarter of 8 = $\boxed{}$
3. one-quarter of 20 = $\boxed{}$
4. one-third of 9 = $\boxed{}$
5. one-half of 120 = $\boxed{}$
6. one-quarter of 40 = $\boxed{}$
7. one-quarter of 100 = $\boxed{}$
8. one-third of 30 = $\boxed{}$
9. one-quarter of 12 = $\boxed{}$
10. one-tenth of 60 = $\boxed{}$
11. one-third of 66 = $\boxed{}$
12. one-tenth of 100 = $\boxed{}$

$\dfrac{1}{3}$ $\dfrac{1}{10}$

E Figure it out. Tick (✓) the correct answer.

1. $(4 + 5) \times 3 =$ a 21 b 24 c 27
2. $(12 - 9) \times 7 =$ a 21 b 24 c 27
3. $(4 \times 4) + 9 =$ a 23 b 25 c 29
4. $(42 \div 6) + 9 =$ a 14 b 16 c 18
5. $(1\cdot2 + 3\cdot1) \times 2 =$ a 8·6 b 6·4 c 4·6
6. $2\cdot25 + 2\cdot5 =$ a 3·75 b 4·75 c 3·3
7. $1\cdot3 + 2\cdot3 + 2\cdot3 =$ a 5·3 b 5·6 c 5·9
8. $(\frac{1}{3} \text{ of } 51) + 1 =$ a 16 b 17 c 18
9. $(\frac{1}{4} \text{ of } 32) + 5 =$ a 13 b 16 c 21
10. $3\cdot75 - 1\cdot25 + 3 =$ a 4·25 b 5 c 5·5
11. $(€2\cdot50 - €1\cdot30) \times 3 =$ a €2·60 b €2·90 c €3·60
12. $€1\cdot50 + €0\cdot99 + €1\cdot50 =$ a €3·99 b €3·79 c €3·59

A Work it out.

1.	2.	3.	4.	5.
€10·99	€8·07	€20·76	€35·99	€13·40
€14·57	€15·88	€17·10	€35·40	€32·55
+ €63·60	+ €65·90	+ €49·77	+ €12·05	+ €34·99

6.	7.	8.	9.	10.
€9·60	€7·79	€4·56	€6·80	€2·94
x 5	x 4	x 7	x 6	x 5

11.	12.	13.	14.	15.
407	467	99	56	30
− 238	− 208	x 4	x 8	x 7

16.	17.	18.	19.	20.
€3·28	€4·07	€7·39	€7·13	€6·90
+ €4·77	+ €9·35	+ €4·15	+ €4·55	+ €4·99
− €3·99	− €6·44	− €6·08	− €3·56	− €7·08

B Work it out.

1.	2.	3.	4.	5.
600	605	634	723	427
− 423	− 344	− 305	− 500	− 377

6.	7.	8.	9.	10.
422	615	723	408	200
+ 387	+ 193	+ 197	+ 299	+ 437
− 505	− 274	− 606	− 308	− 309

11.	12.	13.	14.	15.
49	92	63	80	96
x 9	x 6	x 5	x 7	x 8

16.	17.	18.	19.	20.
6 ⟌ 8 6 4	7 ⟌ 4 6 2	2 ⟌ 8 3 2	5 ⟌ 4 5 5	8 ⟌ 9 1 2

21.	22.	23.	24.	25.
27·5	19·4	23·5	19·1	20·7
15·6	16·8	41·6	16·9	23·8
+ 14·8	+ 10·6	+ 23·9	+ 33·4	+ 31·6

Unit 10 - Problems

A Figure it out.

1. How many feet and tails altogether on 7 dogs? `35`
2. A television was €480. Ann bought it for $\frac{1}{2}$ price. How much did she pay? € `240`
3. How much for 3 cinema tickets at €1·20 each and 2 bags of popcorn at 50c each? € ___
4. How much change from €10·00 after buying the cinema tickets and the popcorn? € ___
5. Tim shared 26c with 2 friends but kept 2c extra for himself. How much did Tim get? ___ c
6. A farmer lost $\frac{1}{3}$ of her sheep. She now has 6 sheep. How many had she at first? ___
7. There are 24 children in 4th class but $\frac{1}{3}$ did no homework. How many did homework? ___
8. Mum bought three €1·00 cards and three 60c stamps. How much did she spend? € ___
9. There are 8 crayons in a pack. How many in $4\frac{1}{2}$ packs? ___
10. Raffle tickets cost 50c each or 3 for €1. How many could you get for €4·50? ___

B Think it out. Tick (✓) the correct answer.

1. 3 ribbons are 34 cm, 43 cm and 50 cm long. The total length is
   a 93 cm b 1 m 77 cm c 1 m 27 cm

2. A bag has 30 marbles. $\frac{1}{6}$ are pink. How many is that? a 3 b 5 c 6

3. A plane arrives 10 mins late at 4:05 p.m. It should have arrived at
   a 3:55 p.m. b 3:05 p.m. c 4:15 p.m.

4. 4th class has 33 children. 5th class has 4 less. How many in 5th? a 28 b 29 c 37

5. By how much is 567 greater than 321?
   a 186 b 246 c 264

6. Kiwis are 20c each or 6 for €1·00. How much for 13 kiwis?
   a €2·20 b 66c c €2·60

7. Diesel cost €15·50 for 10 litres. How much for 1 litre?
   a €1·05 b €1·50 c €1·55

8. How many legs have 4 chickens and 8 goats? a 32 b 40 c 48

9. What is missing? 69 − 23 ▭ 5 × 9
   a = b < c >

10. A rugby match had 15 players on each team. How many played? a 15 b 17 c 30

C Puzzle it out. Complete the Sudokus using 1, 2, 3 and 4 in each square, row and column.

> Remember! Use each number only once in each square, row and column.

1.

4	1	
		4
2		

2.

	2	3
4	1	
3	2	
		4

3.

	4	3	
3	1	4	2

★ Score each exercise out of 10.

A Tables

1. $7 + 9 =$ ☐

2. ☐ $+ 9 = 15$

3. $4 +$ ☐ $= 14$

4. ☐ $- 7 = 8$

5. $17 - 9 =$ ☐

6. ☐ $\times 6 = 54$

7. $72 \div$ ☐ $= 9$

8. $4 \times$ ☐ $= 28$

9. $9 \times 9 =$ ☐

10. ☐ $\div 7 = 7$

Score ☐

B Computation

1.		8	9	2.		8	3	3.		7	0	4.	€3	8	·9	2	5.			2	9
	−	6	0		×		7						€4	5	·0	8		+		4	8
	2	4	9						+	4	8		+ €1	6	·7	7					
									1	7	7							−		6	6

Give yourself 2 marks for each correct sum.   Score ☐

C Fractions and Decimals... Tick (✓) the correct answer.

1. $4\cdot2 + 3\cdot8 =$ a 5·1 b 6·6 c 8·0

2. $1\cdot6 + 0\cdot9 =$ a 0·5 b 1·5 c 2·5

3. $\frac{1}{3}$ of $60 =$ a 20 b 30 c 120

4. $\frac{1}{2}$ of $10 =$ a 5 b 20 c 50

5. $\frac{1}{6}$ of $24 =$ a 4 b 6 c 8

6. $4\cdot5 - 2 + 1\cdot5 =$ a 4 b 3·5 c 7·5

7. $2 - 1\cdot5 + 0\cdot5 =$ a 0·5 b 1 c 1·5

8. $4\cdot5 - 0\cdot5 + 1\cdot5 =$ a 3·5 b 4·5 c 5·5

9. $2\cdot1 + 2\cdot9 - 1\cdot5 =$ a 2·4 b 3·5 c 5

10. $\frac{1}{6}$ of $36 =$ a 6 b 9 c 12

Score ☐

D Shapes, Measures and Data... Write the times that are fifteen minutes earlier than the times shown.

1. 11:55   ☐ : ☐

2. 8:05   ☐ : ☐

3. 9:35   ☐ : ☐

4. 2:10   ☐ : ☐

5. 12:35   ☐ : ☐

6. 1:05   ☐ : ☐

7. 3:15   ☐ : ☐

8. 10:05   ☐ : ☐

9. 12:45   ☐ : ☐

10. 6:25   ☐ : ☐

Score ☐

E Problem Solving

1. Jane got 25c change from €1 after buying 5 bars. How much was each bar?   ☐

2. Meg ate $\frac{3}{4}$ of a box of crackers and there were 2 left. How many did Meg eat?   ☐

3. Tim has read $\frac{1}{3}$ of a 225-page book. How many pages has he read?   ☐

4. An Early Bird menu costs €19·50. How much for 3 meals?   € ☐

5. Cinema tickets cost €1·50. How many tickets for €9·00?   ☐

Give yourself 2 marks for each correct answer.   Score ☐

Unit 11 - Quick Questions

A Tables

1. 8 + 7 = ☐
2. 9 + 9 = ☐
3. 15 – 9 = ☐

4. 18 – 8 = ☐
5. 10 + 10 = ☐
6. 10 x 7 = ☐

7. 9 x 8 = ☐
8. 4 x 6 = ☐
9. 21 ÷ 3 = ☐

10. 56 ÷ 7 = ☐
11. 63 ÷ 9 = ☐
12. 48 ÷ 4 = ☐

B Calculate.

1. 19 + ☐ = 28
2. 23 + ☐ = 41
3. 43 + ☐ = 64
4. ☐ – 11 = 16

5. 36 – ☐ = 18
6. 51 – ☐ = 25
7. 42 – ☐ = 33
8. (4 x 7) – 3 = ☐

9. (3 x 7) – 7 = ☐
10. (42 ÷ 3) + 2 = ☐
11. (55 ÷ 5) x 2 = ☐
12. (66 ÷ 6) + 1 = ☐

C Numbers... Complete the sequences.

1. 26, 29, 32, ☐, ☐, ☐
2. 13, 18, 23, ☐, ☐, ☐
3. 48, 42, 36, ☐, ☐, ☐
4. 4, 7, 10, ☐, ☐, ☐
5. 44, 40, 36, ☐, ☐, ☐
6. 15, 12, 9, ☐, ☐, ☐

7. 7, 9, 11, ☐, ☐, ☐
8. 45, 40, 35, ☐, ☐, ☐
9. 4·5, 5, 5·5, ☐, ☐, ☐
10. 2·8, 2·7, 2·6, ☐, ☐, ☐
11. 4·2, 4·4, 4·6, ☐, ☐, ☐
12. 6·5, 7, 7·5, ☐, ☐, ☐

D Time... Show the times on the clocks.

1. 5:35

3. 2:50

5. 1:10

7. 6:15

9. 9:20

2. 7:05

4. 10:25

6. 9:45

8. 8:15

10. 4:05

E Figure it out. Use +, –, x or ÷ to complete the number sentences.

1. (3 ☐ 4) ☐ 2 = 24
2. (3 ☐ 10) ☐ 6 = 5
3. (4 ☐ 2) ☐ 9 = 18
4. (7 ☐ 3) ☐ 12 = 33

5. 4·55 ☐ 1·45 = 3·10
6. (30 ☐ 15) ☐ 2 = 30
7. (20 ☐ 4) ☐ 3 = 15
8. 4·5 ☐ 1·5 ☐ 3 = 6

9. (5·5 ☐ 2·5) ☐ 2 = 4
10. (2·25 ☐ 2·75) ☐ 2 = 10
11. (12 ☐ 3) ☐ 5 = 9
12. (18 ☐ 9) ☐ 4 = 6

A Work it out.

1.
```
    5 8
x   2 4
```

2.
```
    6 9
x   4 3
```

3.
```
    8 2
x   3 5
```

4.
```
    6 8
x   2 8
```

5.
```
    9 4
x   1 3
```

6.
```
    6 7
x   1 9
```

7.
```
    9 4
x   3 7
```

8.
```
    5 9
x   3 4
```

9.
```
    3 5
x   4 7
```

10.
```
    8 4
x   2 6
```

11.
```
    6 9 4
-   2 0 9
```

12.
```
    8 3 3
-   2 9 4
```

13.
```
    9 0 1
-   5 2 7
```

14.
```
    5 0 0
-   3 4 6
```

15.
```
    3 7 7
-   2 0 9
```

16.
```
    4 1 7
    2 8 7
+   1 0 9
```

17.
```
    3 0 2
    2 5 5
+   1 8 9
```

18.
```
    3 4 4
    6 0 8
+   4 3 9
```

19.
```
    2 5 9
    4 3 3
+   2 0 0
```

20.
```
    8 9
    9 3 6
+   8 2 5
```

B Work it out.

1.
```
  1 7 8 6
+ 2 6 6 6
```

2.
```
  3 0 8 7
+ 2 8 7 6
```

3.
```
  4 1 2 7
+ 1 7 6 5
```

4.
```
  3 4 5 6
+ 1 9 8 7
```

5.
```
  4 0 0 3
+ 1 8 7 9
```

6.
```
    5 9 9
+   4 0 4

-   6 5 7
```

7.
```
    4 2 9
+   1 5 6

-   4 9 9
```

8.
```
    4 9 9
+   4 7 8

-   5 0 0
```

9.
```
    2 0 7
+   4 9 9

-   3 8 7
```

10.
```
    2 8 9
+   1 8 7

-   4 2 7
```

11.
```
    2 4
x   1 2
```

12.
```
    3 3
x   2 3
```

13.
```
    6 2
x   3 1
```

14.
```
    4 5
x   3 2
```

15.
```
    5 4
x   2 6
```

16. 4) 6 0 9   R

17. 7) 5 5 3

18. 5) 7 8 6   R

19. 3) 4 0 4   R

20. 8) 6 1 6

Unit 11 - Problems

A Figure it out.

There are 120 children in St Patrick's school. The school has 9 teachers. See what you can tell about the school.

1. $\frac{1}{2}$ of the children are boys. How many is that? ☐

2. How many girls are in the school? ☐

3. $\frac{1}{6}$ of all the boys are in 4th class. How many is that? ☐

4. There are 8 girls in 4th class. How many children in 4th class? ☐

5. $\frac{1}{3}$ of all the girls in the school come to school on the bus. How many is that? ☐

6. $\frac{1}{3}$ of all the boys in the school come to school in a car. How many is that? ☐

7. $\frac{1}{3}$ of the teachers walk to school. How many is that? ☐

8. One teacher cycles to school. The others come by car. How many come by car? ☐

9. $\frac{1}{2}$ of the 4th class children have blue eyes. How many children is that? ☐

10. $\frac{1}{6}$ of the 4th class children have brown eyes. How many children is that? ☐

B Think it out. Tick (✓) the correct answer.

1. What length is the side of a square if the perimeter is 32 cm?

   a 8 cm b 16 cm c 64 cm

2. 3 papers cost €5·60. Two cost €1·90 and €2·30. How much was the 3rd?

   a €2·20 b €1·60 c €1·40

3. The Irish flag is made up of equal parts of green, white and gold. What fraction is green? a $\frac{1}{3}$ b $\frac{1}{4}$ c $\frac{1}{2}$

4. ☐ is the same as 0·5. a $\frac{1}{4}$ b $\frac{1}{2}$ c $\frac{3}{4}$

5. 5 bags of popcorn cost €2·00. How much for 7 bags? a €2·40 b €2·70 c €2·80

6. What is the total height in cm of two boys who are 1·23 m and 1·45 m?

   a 268 cm b 2·46 m c 2·68 cm

7. By how much is 90 cm less than 2·36 m?

   a 3·26 m b 1·46 cm c 1·46 m

8. Cáit bought a $\frac{1}{2}$ litre can of lemonade. How many ml is that?

   a 500 ml b 750 ml c 250 ml

9. What is missing? 83 − 32 + 7 = (6 x 9) ☐

   a − 6 b + 4 c − 4

10. A school has 24 children in 4th class. $\frac{1}{4}$ are girls. How many are girls? a 6 b 8 c 16

C Puzzle it out. Do the sums and use the answers to crack the code.

V	578	M	384	C	289	E	980	H	364	L	858	N	722	I	966	U	676	O	836	T	464

If you need to, you can work out these sums in your copy.

1. 42 x 23 = ☐
2. 26 x 33 = ☐
3. 44 x 19 = ☐
4. 34 x 17 = ☐
5. 35 x 28 = ☐
6. 66 x 13 = ☐
7. 26 x 26 = ☐
8. 38 x 19 = ☐
9. 17 x 17 = ☐
10. 26 x 14 = ☐
11. 29 x 16 = ☐
12. 69 x 14 = ☐
13. 24 x 16 = ☐
14. 70 x 14 = ☐

Sum No.	1	2	3	4	5	6	7	8	9	10	11	12	13	14
Answer														
Code														

A Tables

1. $3 + \boxed{} = 11$
2. $11 - \boxed{} = 5$
3. $13 - \boxed{} = 6$
4. $\boxed{} - 8 = 7$
5. $3 \times 6 = \boxed{}$
6. $8 \times \boxed{} = 32$
7. $6 \times \boxed{} = 42$
8. $\boxed{} \div 6 = 5$
9. $48 \div \boxed{} = 6$
10. $\boxed{} \div 8 = 9$

Score $\boxed{}$

B Computation

1.
```
    8 4
    5 8
+ 1 0 6
```

2.
```
    5 6
-   2 8
  2 6 9
```

3.
```
  1 4 0
x       7
```

4.
```
  €3 9 ·5 8
+ €4 4 ·0 3
- €6 0 ·2 4
```

5.
```
  1 2 3
x       8
- 3 0 8
```

Give yourself 2 marks for each correct sum.

Score $\boxed{}$

C Fractions and Decimals

1. $\frac{1}{4}$ of $100 = \boxed{}$
2. 0.6 of $10 = \boxed{}$
3. $\frac{1}{8}$ of $16 = \boxed{}$
4. $4.9 + 0.7 = \boxed{}$
5. $4.6 + 0.3 - 2 = \boxed{}$

6. $2.7 - 1.3 + 1 = \boxed{}$
7. $1.3 + 2.4 = \boxed{}$
8. $3.1 + 4.5 + 0.3 = \boxed{}$
9. $\frac{1}{2}$ of 20 less $\frac{1}{4}$ of $16 = \boxed{}$
10. $\frac{1}{3}$ of 6 plus $\frac{1}{5}$ of $10 = \boxed{}$

Score $\boxed{}$

D Shapes, Measures and Data... Ring the number or amount that does not belong.

1. 0·2 kg,   200 g,   5 kg
2. 30 secs, $\frac{1}{2}$ min,   2 mins
3. 10·1, $\frac{1}{10}$,   0·1
4. 50 cm,   5 km,   0·5 m
5. 0·25 l,   0·5 l,   250 ml

6. $\frac{3}{4}$,   0·34,   0·75
7. 2·5 m,   25 cm,   0·25 m
8. 175 g,   17·5 kg,   0·175 kg
9. 3 mins,   90 secs,   180 secs
10. $\frac{1}{10}$,   0·1,   0·01

Score $\boxed{}$

E Problem Solving... Tick (✓) the correct answer.

1. How many 4s in 31?   a 7   b 8   c 9
2. How many centimetres in 2·40 m?   a 2·4 cm   b 24 cm   c 240 cm
3. By how much is 73 less than 101?   a 24   b 28   c 34
4. What is missing? 27 ÷ 3 ▢ 2 x 4   a >   b =   c <
5. How much for 4 cakes at 99c each?   a €3·96   b €3·99   c €4·99

Give yourself 2 marks for each correct answer.

Score $\boxed{}$

Unit 12 - Quick Questions

A Tables

1. 8 x ☐ = 40
2. ☐ x 7 = 35
3. 10 x ☐ = 70
4. ☐ x 3 = 30
5. 6 x ☐ = 48
6. 4 x ☐ = 32
7. 56 ÷ ☐ = 8
8. ☐ ÷ 8 = 7
9. 60 ÷ ☐ = 10
10. 49 ÷ ☐ = 7
11. ☐ ÷ 9 = 6
12. ☐ ÷ 7 = 8

B Calculate.

1. 63 + 34 = ☐
2. 158 – 23 = ☐
3. 26 + 27 = ☐
4. 52 + 56 = ☐
5. 434 – 123 = ☐
6. (12 x 3) + 1 = ☐
7. (28 ÷ 4) – 2 = ☐
8. 22 + 30 + 16 = ☐
9. 51 + 12 + 25 = ☐
10. 22 + 31 + 14 = ☐
11. 95 ÷ 5 = ☐
12. €☐ – €2·50 = €2·00

C Numbers... Write the largest number or amount.

1. 378, 265, 523, 462 ☐
2. 716, 761, 677, 700 ☐
3. 412, 423, 403, 432 ☐
4. 564, 546, 544, 594 ☐
5. €7·99, €7·59, €9·95, €9·59 €☐
6. €8·41, €8·44, €8·14, €8·11 €☐
7. €1·91, €0·99, €1·11, €1·99 €☐
8. €6·27, €7·62, €7·66, €7·99 €☐
9. 2·25, 3·5, 2·75, 3·25 ☐
10. 5·2, 5·9, 6·01, 6 ☐
11. 3·25, 3·52, 3·55, 3·22 ☐
12. 7·63, 7·36, 7·66, 7·35 ☐

D Fractions

1. $\frac{1}{2}$ of 8 plus $\frac{1}{2}$ of 4 = ☐
2. $\frac{1}{4}$ of 8 plus $\frac{1}{4}$ of 4 = ☐
3. $\frac{1}{2}$ of 16 plus $\frac{1}{4}$ of 8 = ☐
4. $\frac{1}{4}$ of 12 plus $\frac{1}{2}$ of 6 = ☐
5. $\frac{1}{8}$ of 8 plus $\frac{1}{4}$ of 4 = ☐
6. $\frac{1}{3}$ of 9 plus $\frac{1}{2}$ of 4 = ☐

7. $\frac{1}{4}$ of 8 plus $\frac{1}{3}$ of 6 = ☐
8. $\frac{1}{2}$ of 24 plus $\frac{1}{4}$ of 8 = ☐
9. $\frac{1}{4}$ of 12 plus $\frac{1}{3}$ of 12 = ☐
10. $\frac{3}{4}$ of 12 = ☐
11. $\frac{2}{3}$ of 9 = ☐
12. $\frac{2}{3}$ of 12 = ☐

E Figure it out. True (✓) or false (✗)?

1. 72 is divisible by 6. ☐
2. 54 is a multiple of 9. ☐
3. $\frac{1}{3}$ of 204 is 66. ☐
4. $\frac{1}{6}$ of 96 is 16. ☐
5. 33 is a quarter of 99. ☐
6. 8·05 p.m. is lunchtime. ☐
7. A cylinder has a triangular shape. ☐
8. $\frac{1}{2}$ of 18 is the same as 3 x 6. ☐
9. 1·3 + 2·3 – 1 = 2·5 ☐
10. 54 + 32 > 66 + 30 ☐
11. One-sixth of 66 is 6. ☐
12. $\frac{1}{4}$ of €2·40 is €0·60. ☐

Be careful! Some division sums have remainders.

A Work it out.

1.	4 3	2.	3 2	3.	6 1	4.	3 9	5.	5 6
x	7	x	5	x	4	x	8	x	9

6.	7 8	7.	6 8	8.	3 7	9.	9 4	10.	8 8
x	9	x	8	x	7	x	6	x	5

11.	3 8	12.	7 5	13.	4 9	14.	9 6	15.	4 9
x 7 2		x 6 3		x 7 5		x 2 5		x 6 7	

16.	8 1 4	17.	6 8 7	18.	4 5 2 3	19.	4 6 3 2	20.	6 0 3 0
− 2 9 9		− 3 8 4		− 8 1 6		− 2 3 3 2		− 4 0 0 5	

B Work it out.

1.	€4 ·4 9	2.	€4 1 ·2 3	3.	€2 7 ·8 2	4.	€3 9 ·2 2	5.	€2 3 ·0 8
+ €1 5 ·3 1		+ €4 2 ·0 6		+ €5 6 ·1 2		+ €2 7 ·4 6		+ €6 9 ·9 7	
− €1 7 ·8 8		− €7 1 ·0 2		− €4 9 ·8 7		− €1 6 ·0 7		− €1 6 ·2 3	

6.	€2 2 ·3 2	7.	€6 5 ·7 9	8.	€3 3 ·6 3	9.	€4 8 ·1 3	10.	€4 8 ·1 5
+ €6 9 ·4 8		+ €2 8 ·8 8		+ €2 1 ·3 1		+ €2 9 ·9 2		+ €3 1 ·6 7	
− €3 7 ·6 5		− €1 5 ·7 1		− €4 0 .0 7		− €5 6 ·7 8		− €2 6 ·2 8	

11.	€6 2 ·5 7	12.	€8 7 ·3 4	13.	8	2 5 6	14.	6	1 5 7	15.	9	2 0 3
− €3 2 ·0 8		− €2 1 ·5 0										

16.	3 4	17.	5 2	18.	6 7	19. R	5 7	20. R	2 7
x 4 4		x 3 3		x 2 2		x 4 4		x 5 5	

Unit 12 - Problems

THE FRUIT SHOP

25c	20c	€1·40 per kg	15c	30c	€1·60	€1·20 per kg	35c
5 for €1	3 for 50c		4 for 50c	4 for €1	2 for €3		3 for €1

A How much for the following:

1. 4 apples? € 60
2. 2 kg of grapes? € 240
3. 10 pears? € 2
4. 6 oranges? € 1.60
5. 5 grapefruits € 1.70

6. 2 apples and 4 oranges? € 1.40
7. 8 kiwis and 2 kg bananas? € 2.40
8. 2 pineapples and 1 kg grapes? € 4.00
9. 1 kg grapes and 1 kg bananas? € 2.60
10. 6 pears and 3 grapefruits? € 2.25

B What change will I have from €2·00 after buying:

1. 4 kiwis? €
2. 1 kg of grapes? €
3. 1 kg of bananas? €
4. 8 apples? €
5. 5 grapefruits? €

6. 1 apple and 1 pineapple? €
7. 5 oranges? €
8. 3 apples and 4 oranges? €
9. 5 pears and 4 oranges? €
10. 6 kiwis and 1 apple? €

C Saturday Shopping

On Saturday Mr White, Mr Green and Mr Brown went to the fruit shop. They had €10 each. When they finished shopping, Mr Green had €1·90 left, Mr Brown had €1·20 left and Mr White had only €0·40 left. Find the total price of each shopping bill and put the correct name with each list.

List 1		List 2		List 3	
3 kg grapes	€ 3.60	7 grapefruits	€	1 pineapple	€
1 pineapple	€1,60	6 pears	€	4 apples	€
6 oranges	€1,60	2 kg bananas	€	3 kg grapes	€
6 apples	€ 1.60	1 kg grapes	€	5 grapefruits	€
8 kiwis	€ 1.00	8 oranges	€	2 pears	€
Total	€	Total	€	Total	€
Change from €10·00	€19	Change from €10·00	€	Change from €10·00	€
Whose fruit?	MG	Whose fruit?		Whose fruit?	

Unit 12 - Check-up

A Tables

1. $5 + 8 =$ ☐   4. $17 -$ ☐ $= 10$ 7. $7 \times 9 =$ ☐   10. $20 \div$ ☐ $= 5$

2. ☐ $+ 7 = 16$ 5. $17 -$ ☐ $= 8$ 8. ☐ $\times 8 = 56$

3. $5 +$ ☐ $= 14$ 6. ☐ $- 5 = 6$ 9. $36 \div 4 =$

Score ☐

B Computation

1.	4	9	1			9	2	0	3.		m	cm	4.					5.		6	5	0
	3	0	2								2	7	3		€4	·0	7				2	7	3
	+	2	7		x			3				3	9					+		2	7	3
										+	4	4	0		x		6			–	3	0	0

Give yourself 2 marks for each correct sum. **Score** ☐

C Fractions and Decimals

1. $0·4 +$ ☐ $= 1$ 5. $0·1 +$ ☐ $= 1$ 9. $0·9 +$ ☐ $= 1$

2. $\frac{3}{10} +$ ☐ $= 1$ 6. $\frac{1}{8} +$ ☐ $= 1$ 10. $\frac{7}{10} +$ ☐ $= 1$

3. $0·7 +$ ☐ $= 1$ 7. $0·5 +$ ☐ $= 1$

4. $\frac{5}{8} +$ ☐ $= 1$ 8. $\frac{3}{4} +$ ☐ $= 1$

Score ☐

D Shapes, Measures and Data

Answer the questions.

1. I get €6·00 pocket money each week and I save one-third. How much do I save? € ☐

2. If bananas are 40c each or 3 for €1·00, how much for 10 bananas? € ☐

Ring the correct measure.

3. 1·5 kg or 1·5 km of meat

4. 0·5 l or 0·5 m of milk

5. 10 kg or 10 km journey

Give yourself 2 marks for each correct answer. **Score** ☐

E Problem Solving

There are 20 dogs in a dog home. One-quarter of them are corgis and half of them are poodles. Half of the poodles wear red collars. The 4 biggest dogs each drink 500 ml of water every morning. Each dog gets 3 bones a week. $\frac{1}{10}$ of the dogs have only three legs.

1. How many corgis are there? ☐

2. How many poodles wear red collars? ☐

3. How many litres of water in total do the 4 biggest dogs drink each morning? ☐ l

4. How many bones in total are needed each week? ☐

5. How many dogs have only three legs? ☐

Give yourself 2 marks for each correct answer. **Score** ☐

Unit 13 - Quick Questions

A Tables

1. 10 + ☐ = 19
2. 9 + ☐ = 18
3. 17 − 9 = ☐
4. 11 − 4 = ☐
5. 8 + ☐ = 15
6. 6 x 7 = ☐
7. 6 x ☐ = 48
8. 4 x 7 = ☐
9. 36 ÷ 3 = ☐
10. 56 ÷ ☐ = 8
11. ☐ ÷ 9 = 7
12. 48 ÷ ☐ = 6

B Calculate.

1. 71 + 29 = ☐
2. 88 − 25 = ☐
3. 94 − 32 = ☐
4. 1·5 − 0·5 = ☐
5. 440 ÷ 4 = ☐
6. 69 + 13 = ☐
7. 2·5 − 2 = ☐
8. €4·27 + €4·13 = €☐
9. 145 + 234 = ☐
10. €3·53 + €☐ = €5·00
11. €☐ + €1·01 = €3·00
12. ☐ − 2·5 = 1·5

C Numbers... Are these numbers > (greater than), < (less than) or = (equal to) each other?

1. $\frac{1}{4}$ of 8 ☐ $\frac{1}{2}$ of 10
2. $\frac{1}{3}$ of 9 ☐ $\frac{1}{2}$ of 4
3. $\frac{1}{4}$ of 12 ☐ $\frac{1}{3}$ of 9
4. $\frac{1}{2}$ of 6 ☐ $\frac{1}{4}$ of 12
5. (2 x 3) + 10 ☐ 20
6. (3 x 10) − 5 ☐ 22
7. (11 x 2) + 1 ☐ 5 x 5
8. 2·5 + 2 + 1 ☐ 7
9. 1 + 0·5 + 0·5 ☐ 2·5
10. 0·25 + 0·25 + 0·25 ☐ 0·65
11. €2·20 + €10·00 ☐ €13·00
12. €5·20 − €1·10 ☐ €4·60

D Money... Find the cost of each shopping list.

 Nuts (N) = 10c   Grapes (G) = 15c   Cheese (C) = 25c

1. 1N + 1G + 1C = €☐
2. 1N + 1G + 2C = €☐
3. 1N + 3G + 2C = €☐
4. 4N + 2G + 1C = €☐
5. 2N + 2G + 2C = €☐
6. 1N + 2G + 2C = €☐
7. 1G + 3C = €☐
8. 4N + 4G = €☐
9. 2N + 3C = €☐
10. 3N + 2G + 1C = €☐
11. 5G + 1C = €☐
12. 10N + 3C = €☐

E Figure it out. Tick (✓) the correct answer.

1. (23 x 2) + 2 =   a 44   b 46   c 48
2. (24 ÷ 4) x 2 =   a 8   b 10   c 12
3. (4 x 8) x 3 =   a 96   b 35   c 95
4. (33 ÷ 3) x 7 =   a 44   b 77   c 99
5. $\frac{1}{5}$ of 45 =   a 5   b 7   c 9
6. $\frac{3}{4}$ of 28 =   a 7   b 14   c 21
7. 0·1 of 37 =   a 3·07   b 3·7   c 3·77
8. (1·2 + 3·1) x 2 =   a 8·4   b 8·6   c 8·8

9. €3·55 − €1·99 + €2·00 =
   a €3·56   b €6·99   c €7·54
10. (€0·99 x 3) + €1·00 =
   a €2·97   b €3·97   c €2·99
11. 24 g + 123 g + 150 g =
   a 197 g   b 273 g   c 297 g
12. 2 m 35 cm + 1 m 99 cm =
   a 334 cm   b 434 cm   c 444 cm

Be careful! Some division sums have remainders.

A Work it out.

1.	2.	3.	4.	5.
6 7 5	6 8 8	3 5 0	1 0 7 7	2 5 6 4
3 1 4	4 1 2	6 2 8	2 8 5 2	2 0 6 7
+ 2 6 0	+ 2 0 0	+ 2 7 8	+ 4 7 3	+ 1 0 9 9

6.	7.	8.	9.	10.
€7 6 ·7 6	€8 0 ·5 9	8 1 2	7 1 9	6 0 8
− €3 6 ·4 8	− €6 3 ·0 1	− 4 7 5	− 6 6 6	− 3 7 7

11.	12.	13.	14.	15.
€3 ·2 4	€2 ·4 5	€3 ·5 6	€7 ·3 2	€6 ·5 9
x 5	x 4	x 8	x 8	x 1 0

16.	17.	18.	19.	20.
3 7 8	2 3 9	3 0 6	6 4 1	5 3 6
4 0 9	4 5 4	4 1 4	1 4 7	4 4 6
+ 2 3 3	+ 2 7 8	+ 2 5 6	+ 2 0 9	+ 2 0 0

B Work it out.

1.	2.	3.	4.	5.
8 7	6 9	3 7	9 9	8 4
x 5 6	x 5 6	x 4 6	x 2 3	x 3 9

6.	7.	8.	9.	10.
8)7 6 8	7)6 2 5	8)4 0 7	4)7 9 5	7)6 5 4
	R	R	R	R

11.	12.	13.	14.	15.
9)6 3 9	7)8 3 3	6)5 0 4	9)6 1 2	8)9 0 4

16.	17.	18.	19.	20.
1 8	7 2	2 4 3	3 5	1 4 8
4 _ 0	4 _ 0	1 3	_ 0 9	4 0
+ _ 3 3	+ 1 7 7	+ _ 2 3	+ 2 _ 4	+ _ 3 3
9 9 9	9 9 9	9 9 9	8 8 1	7 8 8

A Figure it out.

1. How many eyes and ears altogether have 11 children? ☐

2. Apples cost 22c. Bananas cost 15c. How much for 3 apples and 2 bananas? € ☐

3. Jed goes up and down a stairs with 22 steps twice a day. How many steps a day? ☐

4. Jane had €3·00 but spent €1·10. How much has she left? € ☐

5. Santa left 7 sweets in each of 4 children's stockings. How many sweets altogether? ☐

6. John had 20 marbles. He gave 5 away and bought 8 more. How many has he now? ☐

7. Milk is 40c a carton. How many cartons could you buy with €2·50? ☐

8. Molly's watch is 10 mins slow. It says 2:45 p.m. What is the correct time? ☐ p.m.

9. A farm has 5 chickens, 11 ducks and 6 turkeys. How many legs on all the birds? ☐

10. Joy is 2 years younger than Jane. Together their age is 16. What age is Joy? ☐

B Think it out. Tick (✔) the correct answer.

1. There are 40 apples in a box. $\frac{1}{4}$ are red. How many is that? a 4 b 10 c 20

2. A shop has 25 apples, 16 kiwis and 33 pears. How many pieces of fruit in total?
   a 64 b 74 c 84

3. Seán ran for 50 mins. He finished at 4:00 p.m. When did he begin?
   a 3:10 p.m. b 3:50 p.m. c 4:50 p.m.

4. 6 litres of milk cost €10·20. How much for 1 litre? a €1·20 b €4·20 c €1·70

5. How much would a €20 jumper cost in a sale with $\frac{1}{4}$ off? a €10 b €15 c €16

6. How many sides altogether in 1 rectangle and 1 triangle? a 3 b 4 c 7

7. By how much is 336 less than 678?
   a 324 b 332 c 342

8. Raffle tickets are 50c each or 12 for €5·00. How much for 25?
   a €5·50 b €10·50 c €12·50

9. What is missing? 333 − 12 ☐ 300 + 32
   a > b < c =

10. A ribbon is 1 m long. How much is left after using 55 cm?
    a 45 cm b 55 cm c 1 m 55 cm

C Puzzle it out. Use the 100-square to complete the tasks.

1. Ring every 4th number, starting with 3.

2. Find 5 multiples of 6. ☐, ☐, ☐, ☐, ☐

3. What number is 23 greater than 46? ☐

4. Put a line through every 9th number, starting with 2.

5. Find 5 multiples of 7. ☐, ☐, ☐, ☐, ☐

6. Start at 67 and count back 18 to ☐.

7. Put an x on any number that is a multiple of 12.

8. Write four numbers that divide evenly into 18.
   ☐, ☐, ☐, ☐

1	2	3	4	5	6	7	8	9	10
11	12	13	14	15	16	17	18	19	20
21	22	23	24	25	26	27	28	29	30
31	32	33	34	35	36	37	38	39	40
41	42	43	44	45	46	47	48	49	50
51	52	53	54	55	56	57	58	59	60
61	62	63	64	65	66	67	68	69	70
71	72	73	74	75	76	77	78	79	80
81	82	83	84	85	86	87	88	89	90
91	92	93	94	95	96	97	98	99	100

Unit 13 - Check-up

A   Tables

1. 7 + 8 = ☐
2. ☐ + 4 = 12
3. 9 + 7 = ☐
4. ☐ − 7 = 12
5. 13 − 9 = ☐
6. ☐ x 7 = 56
7. 63 ÷ 9 = ☐
8. 4 x ☐ = 24
9. 9 x ☐ = 45
10. ☐ ÷ 7 = 8

Score ☐

B   Computation

1.		6	0	2.		8	5	3.		6	8	4.	€9	·2	0	5.		6	7
	−	3	8		x		7						€3	6	·4	5		+	5	9
		2	4	6					+	2	4		+ €4	8	·0	9				
									1	7	1							−	8	7

Give yourself 2 marks for each correct sum.

Score ☐

C   Fractions and Decimals... Tick (✓) the correct answer.

1. 3·7 + 2·6 =   a 5·1   b 5·13   c 6·3
2. 5·3 − 0·5 =   a 4·8   b 5·3   c 5·8
3. ¼ of 8·4 =   a 2·1   b 2·2   c 4·2
4. ⅕ of 100 =   a 20   b 50   c 200
5. ⅛ of 16 =   a 2   b 4   c 8

6. 2 + 1·5 + 1 =   a 3   b 3·5   c 4·5
7. 3·4 − 0·2 + 2 =   a 5·4   b 5·2   c 7·4
8. 2 − 0·5 − 1 =   a 0·5   b 1   c 1·5
9. 1·6 + 1·2 + 1·1 =   a 2·8   b 3·7   c 3·9
10. ½ of 6·2 =   a 3·1   b 12·4   c 32

Score ☐

D   Shapes, Measures and Data

Write in metres and centimetres.

1. 274 cm = ☐ m ☐ cm
2. 604 cm = ☐ m ☐ cm
3. 311 cm = ☐ m ☐ cm

Answer the questions.

4. €3·07 and €1·65 = € ☐
5. €1·29 and €1·85 = € ☐

Give yourself 2 marks for each correct answer.

Score ☐

E   Problem Solving

1. A bus travelled from 10:15 a.m. to 11:55 a.m. How long was the trip? ☐ mins

2. 3 boys have a total age of 19 years. What age is Ben, if Jim is 4 and Tom is 7? ☐

3. A farmer shares a 354 kg bag of nuts equally between 3 sheep. How much does each get? ☐ kg

4. A book is €4·40 in one shop and one and a half times as much in another shop.

   How much is the book in the second shop? € ☐

5. Sweets are 2c each or 12 for 20c. How much for 27 sweets? € ☐

Give yourself 2 marks for each correct answer.   Score ☐

A Tables

1. 5 x ☐ = 40
2. ☐ x 8 = 64
3. 9 x ☐ = 72
4. ☐ x 10 = 60
5. 7 x ☐ = 63
6. 4 x ☐ = 36
7. 36 ÷ ☐ = 4
8. ☐ ÷ 10 = 8
9. 63 ÷ ☐ = 9
10. 36 ÷ ☐ = 9
11. ☐ ÷ 6 = 4
12. ☐ ÷ 3 = 12

B Calculate.

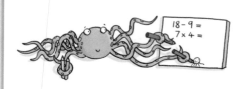

1. 45 + 146 = ☐
2. 35 + ☐ = 62
3. 39 + ☐ = 71
4. 49 − ☐ = 33
5. 94 − ☐ = 31
6. 23 x 3 = ☐
7. (12 x 7) − 3 = ☐
8. 480 ÷ 4 = ☐
9. 606 ÷ 6 = ☐
10. (36 ÷ 4) + 2 = ☐
11. (16 ÷ 4) + 3 = ☐
12. €3·66 − €2·34 = € ☐

C Numbers... Are these numbers > (greater than) or < (less than) each other?

1. 9 + 8 + 20 ☐ 11 + 11 + 11
2. 14 + 10 + 20 ☐ 31 + 1 + 10
3. 15 + 8 + 20 ☐ 12 + 8 + 20
4. 8 + 8 + 15 ☐ 10 + 8 + 20
5. (22 x 3) + 3 ☐ 12 + 8 + 20
6. 3 x 13 ☐ 10 x 4
7. 22 + 8 + 20 ☐ 54
8. (3·4 + 1·5) + 1 ☐ 5
9. 25 + 40 ☐ 30 + 30
10. $\frac{1}{2}$ ☐ $\frac{3}{4}$
11. 3·25 + 1 ☐ 2·5 + 2
12. €4·99 − €3·00 ☐ €5·00 − €0·50

D Money... Write as euros and cents.

1. 923c € ☐
2. 406c € ☐
3. 200c € ☐
4. 87c € ☐
5. 426c € ☐
6. 147c € ☐
7. 316c € ☐
8. 510c € ☐
9. 601c € ☐
10. 311c € ☐
11. 938c € ☐
12. 705c € ☐

E Figure it out. Use +, −, X or ÷ to complete the number sentences.

1. (6 ☐ 2) ☐ 3 = 24
2. (12 ☐ 2) ☐ 6 = 60
3. (30 ☐ 6) ☐ 3 = 2
4. 2 ☐ 2 ☐ 2 = 8
5. (€3·33 ☐ 3) ☐ €0·01 = €10·00
6. (€6·99 ☐ 3) ☐ €2·00 = €4·33
7. 6 ☐ 10 ☐ 2 = 30
8. 7·5 ☐ 2·5 ☐ 2 = 7
9. 3 ☐ 5 ☐ 2 = 30
10. (16 ☐ 4) ☐ 3 = 7
11. (24 ☐ 3) ☐ 1 = 9
12. 100 ☐ 10 = 10

A Work it out.

1.	3 7 x 5 2	2.	5 9 x 3 6	3.	4 9 x 3 5	4.	4 7 x 3 6	5.	7 5 x 2 7

6.	2 6 5 3 – 1 9 9 9	7.	4 6 2 8 – 2 0 8 8	8.	2 1 7 6 – 1 7 6 8	9.	6 1 2 8 – 1 6 4 4	10.	2 7 1 4 – 1 6 7 5

11.	7) 7 3 5	12.	4) 4 2 4	13.	9) 2 0 7	14.	7) 3 2 2	15.	5) 1 6 5

16.	2 3 ·9 2 5 ·6 + 3 2 ·4 — – 4 5 ·6	17.	1 8 ·7 4 0 ·9 + 3 5 ·4 — – 3 6 ·6	18.	3 9 ·4 1 5 ·6 + 1 6 ·7 — – 1 9 ·9	19.	4 6 ·2 2 2 ·8 + 3 0 ·4 — – 5 1 ·6	20.	6 2 ·7 1 5 ·6 + 1 2 ·8 — – 3 0 ·7

B Work it out.

1.	€2 2 ·3 2 €1 4 ·5 5 + €3 4 ·9 5	2.	€4 5 ·5 4 €1 6 ·3 7 + €2 0 ·1 1	3.	€3 7 ·8 2 €1 4 ·0 7 + €1 7 ·9 9	4.	€3 9 ·0 4 €2 4 ·5 6 + €1 1 ·5 9	5.	€2 8 ·8 2 €3 7 ·8 8 + €5 ·3 6

6.	€7 3 ·8 6 – €4 2 ·6 5	7.	€1 9 ·6 6 – €6 ·5 6	8.	€4 9 ·1 1 – €3 2 ·5 5	9.	€4 ·3 3 x 6	10.	€3 ·0 7 x 8

11.	8) 3 0 7	12.	9) 4 2 8	13.	6) 5 2 2	14.	7) 3 0 8	15.	4) 8 2 3

16.	R 3 6 x 2 6	17.	R 6 5 x 2 3	18.	4 1 x 3 8	19.	6 3 x 5 2	20.	R 4 5 x 2 8

Unit 14 - Problems

A Figure it out.

4th class had a cake sale. There are 32 children in 4th class. What can you tell?

1. All the children brought €2·00 each to the cake sale. How much in total? € [ ]

2. 8 children spent all of their money. How much money was that? € [ ]

3. Drinks were 50c. $\frac{1}{2}$ of the children bought a drink. How much was that? € [ ]

4. $\frac{1}{4}$ of the children brought in 10 small cakes each. How many was that? [ ]

5. Pink buns were sold for 20c each. How much for 25 pink buns? € [ ]

6. There are 21 boys in the class. All the girls bought a pink bun. How much in total? € [ ]

7. All large cakes were sold for €2·20 each. How much for 5 large cakes? € [ ]

8. The teacher bought a large cake, a drink and a pink bun. How much in total? € [ ]

9. 100 raffle tickets were sold for 50c each. How much in total? € [ ]

10. $\frac{1}{3}$ of the boys bought one raffle ticket each. How much in total? € [ ]

B Think it out. Tick (✓) the correct answer.

1. Nine thousand, one hundred and seven =
   a 9701 b 9117 c 9107

2. Ice-creams are 30c each or 6 for €1·50. How much for 9?
   a €1·90 b €2·40 c €2·70

3. How much for 5 litres of petrol at €1·90 a litre? a €9·50 b €9·90 c €10·50

4. A boat left at 11:25 a.m. and travelled for 50 mins. It arrived at
   a 11:30 a.m. b 12:05 p.m. c 12:15 p.m.

5. How many 9s in 64? a 6 b 7 c 8

6. How many sides in 1 triangle and 2 rectangles? a 7 b 8 c 11

7. By how much is 299 less than 506?
   a 203 b 207 c 215

8. What is $\frac{1}{6}$ of 18 plus $\frac{1}{8}$ of 16? a 5 b 6 c 7

9. What is missing? 32 ÷ 4 [ ] 42 ÷ 6
   a > b < c =

10. Cows in a field had 28 ears in total. How many cows were there? a 7 b 14 c 56

C Puzzle it out. Do the sums and complete the cross-number puzzle.

Across
1. 18 x 16 = [ ]
3. 999 − 77 = [ ]
6. 5 x 9 = [ ]
8. 879 − 242 = [ ]
10. 77 x 4 = [ ]
11. 12 x 7 = [ ]
13. 114 ÷ 6 = [ ]
14. 143 x 3 = [ ]
16. 387 + 682 = [ ]
18. 31 x 6 = [ ]
19. 113 x 3 = [ ]

Down
1. 7 x 4 = [ ]
2. 109 − 23 = [ ]
3. 276 − 179 = [ ]
4. 1007 + 1342 = [ ]
5. 4203 + 3611 = [ ]
7. 171 x 3 = [ ]
9. 88 x 4 = [ ]
12. 3196 + 1672 = [ ]
13. 3045 − 1302 = [ ]
15. 104 x 9 = [ ]
17. 10 x 9 = [ ]

If you need to, you can work out these sums in your copy.

A Tables

1. 8 + ☐ = 17   4. ☐ − 8 = 13   7. ☐ x 8 = 72   10. 48 ÷ ☐ = 6

2. ☐ − 6 = 9   5. 3 x 9 = ☐   8. ☐ ÷ 6 = 9

3. 15 − ☐ = 8   6. 8 x ☐ = 64   9. ☐ ÷ 6 = 7

Score ☐

B Computation

1.
```
      1 2 7
    + 3 1 9
      6 5 2
```

2.
```
      1 8
  -   4 0
    1 2 8
```

3.
```
    2 4
  x    8
```

4.
```
  €3 4 ·0 6
 -€1 4 ·6 7
 +€2 4 ·8 2
```

5.
```
        3 9
  x        9
  -   2 0 4
```

Give yourself 2 marks for each correct answer.   Score ☐

C Fractions and Decimals

1. $\frac{1}{5}$ of 25 = ☐

2. $\frac{1}{3}$ of 24 = ☐

3. $\frac{3}{4}$ of 4·4 = ☐

4. 4·7 + 0·8 = ☐

5. 5·4 + 0·5 − 1 = ☐

6. 3·5 + 1·2 + 0·3 = ☐

7. 3·6 − 1·3 + 1 = ☐

8. 1·9 + 2·3 + 1·2 = ☐

9. $\frac{1}{5}$ of 15 less $\frac{1}{4}$ of 4 = ☐

10. $\frac{1}{3}$ of 6 plus $\frac{1}{4}$ of 8 = ☐

Score ☐

D Shapes, Measures and Data... Write **speed**, **weight**, **length**, **capacity** or **distance**.

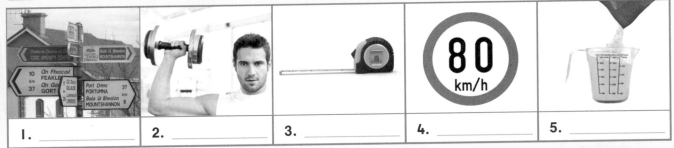

1. _____   2. _____   3. _____   4. _____   5. _____

Give yourself 2 marks for each correct answer.   Score ☐

E Problem Solving... Tick (✔) the correct answer.

1. How many 6s in 52?   a 7   b 8   c 9

2. How many faces on a cube?   a 6   b 8   c 10

3. By how much is 311 greater than 240?   a 51   b 69   c 71

4. What is missing? 37 − 8 ☐ 3 x 7   a >   b =   c <

5. How much for 6 stamps at 60c each?   a €2·80   b €3·00   c €3·60

Give yourself 2 marks for each correct answer.   Score ☐

A Tables

1. $4 +$ ☐ $= 11$
2. ☐ $+ 9 = 15$
3. $19 -$ ☐ $= 10$
4. $18 -$ ☐ $= 8$
5. $9 +$ ☐ $= 15$
6. $9 \times$ ☐ $= 63$
7. $7 \times 8 =$ ☐
8. $6 \times$ ☐ $= 66$
9. $42 \div 6 =$ ☐
10. $55 \div 5 =$ ☐
11. $63 \div$ ☐ $= 7$
12. $48 \div 6 =$ ☐

B Calculate.

1. $26 +$ ☐ $= 42$
2. $34 +$ ☐ $= 89$
3. $27 +$ ☐ $= 51$
4. $75 -$ ☐ $= 50$
5. $31 -$ ☐ $= 17$
6. $42 -$ ☐ $= 26$
7. $(4 \times 6) + 3 =$ ☐
8. $(4 \times 4) + 8 =$ ☐
9. $312 \div 3 =$ ☐
10. $(12 \div 4) + 6 =$ ☐
11. $1 \cdot 42 +$ ☐ $= 3 \cdot 63$
12. $9 \cdot 34 - 6 \cdot 12 =$ ☐

C Numbers... Complete the sequences.

1. 60, 50, 40, ☐, ☐, ☐
2. 3·3, 4·4, 5·5, ☐, ☐, ☐
3. 34, 30, 26, ☐, ☐, ☐
4. 4, 8, 12, ☐, ☐, ☐
5. 35, 40, 45, ☐, ☐, ☐
6. 61, 56, 51, ☐, ☐, ☐
7. 12, 16, 20, ☐, ☐, ☐
8. 23, 26, 29, ☐, ☐, ☐
9. 9·6, 9·3, 9, ☐, ☐, ☐
10. 4·7, 4·2, 3·7, ☐, ☐, ☐

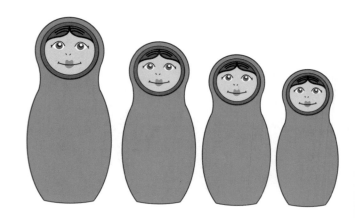

11. 1·25, 1·75, 2·25, ☐, ☐, ☐
12. 9·5, 9, 8·5, ☐, ☐, ☐

D Fractions

1. $\frac{1}{3}$ of 15 = ☐
2. $\frac{1}{4}$ of 16 = ☐
3. $\frac{1}{4}$ of 40 = ☐
4. $\frac{1}{2}$ of 40 = ☐
5. $\frac{3}{4}$ of 40 = ☐
6. $\frac{1}{3}$ of 9 = ☐
7. $\frac{1}{10}$ of 70 = ☐
8. $\frac{1}{4}$ of 40 = ☐
9. $\frac{1}{3}$ of 18 = ☐
10. $\frac{1}{10}$ of 120 = ☐
11. $\frac{1}{5}$ of 15 = ☐
12. $\frac{2}{3}$ of 15 = ☐

E Figure it out. True (✓) or false (✗)?

1. 108 is divisible by 12. ☐
2. 189 is a multiple of 7. ☐
3. $\frac{1}{3}$ of 261 is 88. ☐
4. ($\frac{1}{4}$ of 44) plus 5 is 18. ☐
5. 45 is one-quarter of 90. ☐
6. The sun shines at 10:45 p.m. ☐
7. A rectangle is the same as a square. ☐
8. $\frac{1}{2}$ is the same as 0·5. ☐
9. $3 \cdot 25 + 2 \cdot 25 + 1 \cdot 25 = 7 \cdot 75$ ☐
10. $567 < 765$ ☐
11. $\frac{2}{3}$ of 9 is 3. ☐
12. €4·25 x 4 = €17·00 ☐

Be careful! Some division sums have remainders.

Unit 15 - Simply Sums

A Work it out.

1. 6)4 0 3   2. 5)6 1 2   3. 7)3 9 9   4. 4)5 1 7   5. 7)6 2 8
        R   R   R   R

6.   4 7 3   7.   4 7 2   8.   4 9 0   9.   5 2 8   10.   6 0 1
   −   2 9 1   −   2 8 8   −   3 0 7   −   3 9 9   −   4 3 0

11.   7 3   12.   5 6   13.   6 4   14.   4 8   15.   3 7
      x   4 2   x   2 9   x   2 6   x   2 2   x   2 8

16. 3)7 1 9   17. 8)7 4 4   18. 7)8 0 5   19. 6)8 3 2   20. 9)7 4 9
        R   R   R

B Work it out.

1.   7 2 9   2.   5 1 1   3.   5 1 7   4.   3 0 7   5.   8 8 7
   −   2 3 7   −   3 6 5   −   2 7 6   −   2 3 0   −   5 7 5

6.   4 7 6   7.   1 9 8   8.   4 7 3   9.   7 0 4   10.   5 0 1
   −   2 8 8   −   9 9   −   1 2 9   −   6 9 0   −   3 4 8

11. 6)6 8 9   12. 5)6 0 8   13. 7)2 1 7   14. 9)4 8 6   15. 8)7 2 6
        R   R   R

16.   4 2   17.   2 4   18.   5 4   19.   4 5   20.   4 6
      x   4 3   x   6 5   x   6 3   x   2 3   x   2 5

21.   6 0   22.   5 0   23.   7 4   24.   5 6   25.   9 2
      x   1 5   x   2 7   x   4 7   x   3 5   x   1 8

61

Unit 15 - Problems

A Shopping for Goldfish

Tom, Jenny and Adam got €10·00 each from Uncle Pat. They went to the pet shop to buy some goldfish. Jenny spent €6·45. Tom spent €9·50. They spent €21·95 altogether.

1. How many fish in the fish tank? ☐

2. How many (a) red goldfish? ☐ (b) yellow goldfish? ☐ (c) panda fish? ☐
   (d) bubble-eye fish? ☐

3. Number the fish from dearest to cheapest (1 = dearest and 4 = cheapest).
   (a) yellow ☐ (b) red ☐ (c) panda ☐ (d) bubble-eye ☐

4. How much for (a) three panda fish? €☐ (b) two bubble-eye fish? €☐

5. Which child spent most? ☐

6. How much change did Jenny get from €10·00? €☐

7. One child bought the round bowl and 4 yellow fish. Who was that? ☐

8. Tom bought 2 tins of fish food, 5 red fish and 4 yellow fish. He spent the rest of his money on panda fish. How many panda fish did he buy? ☐

B Imagine you are in the pet shop.

1. How much would you pay for (a) all the red fish? €☐ (b) all the yellow fish? €☐ (c) all the panda fish? €☐ (d) all the bubble-eye fish? €☐

2. How many panda fish could you get for €3·50? ☐

3. How much for: (a) one tin of food and three yellow fish? €☐ (b) a circular fish bowl and two red fish? €☐ (c) one of each kind of fish? €☐

4. How much more would you pay for the tank than for the bowl? €☐

5. How much for 2 yellow and 2 red fish if the fish are half price? €☐

6. If you had €10·00 to spend in this pet shop, what would you buy?

   You will need food and a bowl or tank!

   _____ €____
   _____ €____
   _____ €____
   _____ €____
   _____ €____
   _____ €____
   TOTAL €____

Unit 15 – Check-up

A Tables

1. $9 + 9 =$ ☐
2. ☐ $+ 9 = 17$
3. $6 +$ ☐ $= 15$

4. $13 -$ ☐ $= 4$
5. $20 -$ ☐ $= 10$
6. ☐ $- 9 = 8$

7. $6 \times 6 =$ ☐
8. $8 \times$ ☐ $= 32$
9. $40 \div$ ☐ $= 4$

10. ☐ $\div 8 = 5$

Score ☐

B Computation

1.		9	5		2.	3	6	0	6		3.		m	cm		4.		€9	·3	4		5.		7	0	2
			3	4									2	6	7		−	€8	·9	9			+	2	9	9
	+	2	8			x			4				3	0	4								−	4	7	0
		8	5	5								+	4	1	9		x			9						

Give yourself 2 marks for each correct sum.

Score ☐

C Fractions and Decimals

1. $0.7 +$ ☐ $= 3$
2. $1.6 +$ ☐ $= 3$
3. $2.3 +$ ☐ $= 3$
4. $0.8 +$ ☐ $= 3$
5. $0.5 +$ ☐ $= 3$

$\dfrac{1}{7}$

6. $1.5 +$ ☐ $= 3$
7. $2.6 +$ ☐ $= 3$
8. $2.5 +$ ☐ $= 3$
9. $1.4 +$ ☐ $= 3$
10. $2.7 +$ ☐ $= 3$

Score ☐

D Shapes, Measures and Data

I had €10·00 but I only have €3·60 left.
How much did I spend?

1. €2·20 and € ☐
2. €3·50 and € ☐

Which measure is greater?

3. m or cm? ☐
4. ml or l? ☐
5. g or kg? ☐

Give yourself 2 marks for each correct answer.

Score ☐

E Problem Solving

20 horses ran in a race. $\frac{1}{2}$ of them fell. The other horses all finished the race. $\frac{1}{4}$ of the jockeys wore red caps. $\frac{1}{10}$ of the jockeys were women and they all finished the race.

1. How many horses fell? ☐
2. How many horses finished the race? ☐
3. How many jockeys wore red caps? ☐
4. How many women rode horses in the race? ☐
5. How many men finished the race? ☐

Give yourself 2 marks for each correct answer.

Score ☐

Unit 16 - Quick Questions

A Tables

1. 7 x ☐ = 35
2. ☐ x 9 = 27
3. 11 x ☐ = 88
4. ☐ x 4 = 48
5. 8 x ☐ = 64
6. 6 x ☐ = 54
7. 56 ÷ ☐ = 8
8. ☐ ÷ 12 = 3
9. 32 ÷ ☐ = 4
10. 49 ÷ ☐ = 7
11. ☐ ÷ 12 = 5
12. ☐ ÷ 6 = 9

B Calculate.

1. 206 + 31 + 22 = ☐
2. 105 + 40 + 31 = ☐
3. 144 + 13 + 12 = ☐
4. 333 + 50 + 12 = ☐
5. 165 − 132 = ☐
6. 40 x 4 = ☐
7. 52 ÷ 4 = ☐
8. 72 ÷ 3 = ☐
9. (3 x 12) + 14 = ☐
10. (2 x 44) + 13 = ☐
11. 59 − ☐ = 26
12. €3·65 + €4·14 = €☐

C Numbers... Order from largest to smallest.

1. 267, 271, 257   ☐ , ☐ , ☐
2. 345, 234, 456   ☐ , ☐ , ☐
3. 19 − 2, 19 + 2, 19 − 3   ☐ , ☐ , ☐
4. 33 + 5, 38 − 3, 36 + 4   ☐ , ☐ , ☐
5. 34·9, 39·4, 37·9   ☐ , ☐ , ☐
6. 61·8, 68·1, 81·6   ☐ , ☐ , ☐
7. 25·5, 26·1, 21·6   ☐ , ☐ , ☐
8. 16·7, 17·6, 17·7   ☐ , ☐ , ☐
9. 1·3, 1·5, 1·7   ☐ , ☐ , ☐
10. 2·7, 2·3, 2·5   ☐ , ☐ , ☐
11. $\frac{1}{2}$, $\frac{1}{4}$, $\frac{3}{4}$ ☐ , ☐ , ☐
12. 0·5, $\frac{1}{10}$, $\frac{7}{8}$ ☐ , ☐ , ☐

D Time... Write the digital times.

1.    ☐ : ☐
2.    ☐ : ☐
3.    ☐ : ☐
4.    ☐ : ☐
5.    ☐ : ☐
6.    ☐ : ☐
7.    ☐ : ☐
8.    ☐ : ☐
9.    ☐ : ☐
10.    ☐ : ☐

E Figure it out. Tick (✓) the correct answer.

1. 165 + 13 − 55 =   a 97   b 113   c 123
2. 206 − 32 + 26 =   a 200   b 208   c 224
3. (54 ÷ 9) x 2 =   a 6   b 12   c 14
4. (63 ÷ 7) x 3 =   a 12   b 18   c 27
5. (5 x 3) + 3 =   a 12   b 15   c 18
6. (12 x 4) + 2 =   a 46   b 48   c 50
7. (2·3 + 1·2) x 2 =   a 6·5   b 7   c 7·5
8. (5·6 − 3·2) x 2 =   a 2·4   b 4·4   c 4·8
9. $\frac{1}{4}$ of 24 =   a 4   b 6   c 8
10. $\frac{1}{8}$ of 24 =   a 3   b 6   c 8

Be careful! Some division sums have remainders.

A Work it out.

1.
```
      5
    9
  + 7 6
  2 3 4
```

2.
```
        4
      3
  + 4 9
  1 3 8
```

3.
```
      5
    9
  + 8 6
  2 7 5
```

4.
```
          5
        9
  +   8 8
    2 9 9
```

5.
```
        5
      9
  + 7 6
  2 5 7
```

6.
```
  €5 4 ·2 1
- €3 5 ·5 5
```

7.
```
  €4 0 ·1 9
- €3 4 ·8 4
```

8.
```
  €5 7 ·4 4
- €3 4 ·5 5
```

9.
```
  €8 0 ·2 5
- €4 2 ·8 0
```

10.
```
  €3 5 ·2 0
- €2 8 ·3 4
```

11.
```
  €7 ·8 2
x       6
```

12.
```
  €9 ·4 5
x       7
```

13.
```
  €6 ·7 3
x       8
```

14.
```
  €8 ·2 9
x       9
```

15.
```
  €2 ·4 9
x       7
```

16.
```
      3 9
  x 8 4
```

17.
```
      9 4
  x 2 5
```

18.
```
      6 8
  x 4 8
```

19.
```
      8 8
  x 7 4
```

20.
```
      5 3
  x 2 7
```

B Work it out.

1. 6) 7 8 5   R

2. 9) 4 5 7   R

3. 7) 4 4 3   R

4. 5) 8 2 5

5. 8) 6 4 5   R

6.
```
    3 9 7
  + 4 0 2

  - 2 4 4
```

7.
```
    3 7 8
  + 1 6 8

  - 4 1 2
```

8.
```
    3 7 6
  + 1 0 9

  - 2 1 9
```

9.

m	cm
1	09
2	50
+ 1	47

10.

m	cm
1	23
2	10
+ 2	45

11. 8) 3 8 9   R

12. 7) 4 4 2

13. 9) 5 5 2   R

14. 6) 7 3 2

15. 7) 3 6 5   R

16.
```
      7 2
  x 2 4
```

17.
```
      4 5
  x 6 1
```

18.
```
      7 3
  x 2 5
```

19.
```
      8 8
  x 3 6
```

20.
```
      7 4
  x 2 4
```

A Figure it out.

1. There are 144 children in a school. 0·5 of them are boys. How many are girls? ☐
2. Apples are 15c, bananas, 20c and kiwis, 25c. How much will 3 of each cost in total? € ☐
3. Twins were born weighing 2·45 kg and 3·05 kg. What was their total weight? ☐ kg
4. A man wants to share €1263 with his two brothers. How much will each get? € ☐
5. A farmer had 17 calves. He sold 12 and bought 5 more. How many has he now? ☐
6. There are 6 bagels in a pack. How many in $7\frac{1}{2}$ packs? ☐
7. How many 35c bags of crisps can you buy for €4·20? ☐
8. A train left at 7:20 a.m. and arrived at 8:35 a.m. How long was the journey? ☐ mins
9. Bags of potatoes weigh 2·5 kg and cost €1·60. How much for 7·5 kg of potatoes? € ☐
10. The total age of three children is 24. Two are 7 and 11. What age is the other? ☐

B Think it out. Tick (✓) the correct answer.

1. A rectangle is 6 cm wide and 8 cm long. What length is the perimeter?
   a 14 cm b 28 cm c 48 cm

2. 3 boxes weigh 28 kg. A weighs 8 kg. B weighs 6·5 kg. What weight is C?
   a 11·5 kg b 13·5 kg c 14 kg

3. Jim had 18 marbles. 6 were red. What fraction was red? a $\frac{1}{3}$ b $\frac{1}{4}$ c $\frac{1}{6}$

4. Mary had 52 cards but gave $\frac{1}{2}$ to Pat. How many cards has Pat now? a 13 b 26 c 52

5. A pole is $4\frac{1}{4}$ m tall. How many cm is that?
   a 4·25 cm b 4·4 cm c 425 cm

6. 6 bags of oranges cost €12·00. How much for 8 bags? a €16·00 b €18·00 c €20·00

7. How much greater is 1·14 kg than 600 g?
   a 1·64 g b 540 g c 540 kg

8. Rob drank $\frac{3}{4}$ of a litre of milk. How many ml was that? a $\frac{1}{4}$ ml b 75 ml c 750 ml

9. What is missing? 37 − 12 + 6 = 40 − 10
   a + 1 b − 1 c + 5

10. A school has 240 children. 0·5 are girls. How many girls are there?
    a 48 b 120 c 1200

C Puzzle it out. Complete the Sudokus using 1, 2, 3, 4, 5 and 6 in each row and column.

> Remember! Use each number only once in each row and column.

1.

3	2	1			
4	5	6		3	
6	1	2			
	3		1	2	6
	6		3	1	4
			5	6	2

2.

5	6		2		3
1		3		4	
	3		1		2
6		2		5	
	4		5		1
3		1		2	

Unit 16 - Check-up

A Tables

1. $8 + 9 =$ ☐
2. $14 -$ ☐ $= 7$
3. $7 +$ ☐ $= 15$
4. ☐ $- 7 = 9$
5. ☐ $- 9 = 4$
6. ☐ $\div 5 = 7$
7. ☐ $\times 9 = 72$
8. ☐ $\div 7 = 9$
9. ☐ $\times 4 = 36$
10. $54 \div$ ☐ $= 9$

Score ☐

B Computation

1.					2.		8	4	3.		2	1	6	4.	€4	3	·9	9	5.		3	1	4
	−	6	7	8	×			6							€3	7	·1	8		+	2	0	8
		1	2	5						+	1	8	0	+	€1	6	·0	2					
											9	2	3							−	1	7	9

Give yourself 2 marks for each correct sum. Score ☐

C Fractions and Decimals... Tick (✔) the correct answer.

1. $7·2 - 1·3 =$ a ☐ 5·9 b ☐ 6·1 c ☐ 8·5
2. $5·4 + 2·6 =$ a ☐ 7·10 b ☐ 7·2 c ☐ 8
3. $\frac{1}{3}$ of 99 = a ☐ 33 b ☐ 66 c ☐ 132
4. $\frac{1}{10}$ of 70 = a ☐ 7 b ☐ 10 c ☐ 80
5. $\frac{1}{5}$ of 10 = a ☐ 2 b ☐ 5 c ☐ 15

6. $\frac{1}{4}$ of 24 = a ☐ 2 b ☐ 4 c ☐ 6
7. $1·5 + 1·3 + 1·2 =$ a ☐ 3 b ☐ 3·5 c ☐ 4
8. $5 - 3 + 2·5 =$ a ☐ 4 b ☐ 4·5 c ☐ 8·5
9. $6·1 + 1·4 - 2·3 =$ a ☐ 5·2 b ☐ 5·5 c ☐ 9·2
10. $\frac{1}{4}$ of 28 = a ☐ 3 b ☐ 5 c ☐ 7

Score ☐

D Shapes, Measures and Data

1. How much is left from a 500 g bag of sugar if I used 120 g? ☐ g

2. How much is left from a 500 g bag of sugar if I used 325 g? ☐ g

3. What am I? I am a flat, almost round shape. I am not a circle. ☐

4. What am I? I am a common, flat, regular shape. I have no corners. ☐

5. What am I? I look square-ish but only my opposite lines are the same length. ☐

Give yourself 2 marks for each correct answer. Score ☐

E Problem Solving

1. A train travels at 80 km an hour. How long would it take to travel 20 km? ☐ mins

2. There are four children aged 12, 9 and 3-year-old twins. What is their total age? ☐

3. A 1 m 80 cm ribbon was cut in 3 equal pieces. What length is each piece? ☐ cm

4. There are 52 cards in a pack. A quarter are clubs. How many is that? ☐

5. Stickers are 20c each or 6 for €1. How much for 15 stickers? € ☐

Give yourself 2 marks for each correct answer. Score ☐

Unit 17 - Quick Questions

A Tables

1. 9 + 12 = ☐
2. 8 + 9 = ☐
3. 22 – 11 = ☐

4. 16 – ☐ = 6
5. 12 + ☐ = 20
6. 9 x 7 = ☐

7. 5 x 8 = ☐
8. 4 x ☐ = 36
9. 36 ÷ 3 = ☐

10. ☐ ÷ 7 = 5
11. ☐ ÷ 9 = 4
12. ☐ ÷ 4 = 8

B Calculate.

1. 36 + ☐ + 25 = 100
2. 49 + ☐ + 14 = 100
3. 26 + ☐ + 19 = 100
4. 31 + ☐ + 31 = 100

5. 120 – ☐ = 45
6. 110 – ☐ = 69
7. (7 x 6) – 4 = ☐
8. (6 x 9) – 12 = ☐

9. (2 x 34) + 1 = ☐
10. (3 x 23) – 2 = ☐
11. 4·56 – 1·44 = ☐
12. 3·25 – 2·24 = ☐

C Numbers... Complete the tables.

Tables	1	2	3	4	5	6	7	8	9	10
x 4										
x 5										
x 6										
x 8										

D Time... Write the times on the digital clocks.

1. half past three

3:30

4. quarter to two

☐:☐

7. half past eight

☐:☐

10. twenty-five to nine

☐:☐

2. quarter past one

☐:☐

5. twenty past twelve

☐:☐

8. twenty to seven

☐:☐

11. ten past eight

☐:☐

3. half past six

☐:☐

6. ten to four

☐:☐

9. five o'clock

☐:☐

12. twenty-five to ten

☐:☐

E Figure it out. Use +, –, x or ÷ to complete the number sentences.

1. 3 ☐ 2 ☐ 5 = 30
2. 15 ☐ 3 ☐ 5 = 17
3. (44 ☐ 4) ☐ 4 = 15
4. (5 ☐ 5) ☐ 10 = 35
5. (€3·50 ☐ €2·30) ☐ 2 = €2·40
6. (€6·00 ☐ €5·00) ☐ 2 = €0·50

7. (8 ☐ 2) ☐ 5 = 9
8. 2 ☐ 0·5 ☐ 0·4 = 1·1
9. (6 ☐ 4) ☐ 2 = 20
10. (9 ☐ 3) ☐ 3 = 18
11. 6 ☐ 2 ☐ 3 = 7
12. (10 ☐ 5) ☐ 3 = 6

Be careful! Some division sums have remainders.

A Work it out.

1.
```
        5
    8   4
+   9
    2   0   6
```

2.
```
            4
        8   6
+   8
    2   4   4
```

3.
```
    1       5
        8   6
+       9
    3   1   2
```

4.
```
    4   0   0   8
    1   5   1   3
+   2   0   6   6
```

5.
```
    1   0   6   7
    1   0   9   6
+   3   4   5   5
```

6.
```
        8   4
        5   3
        2   6
+   5   7
```

7.
```
        5   8
        3   7
        2   9
+   2   4
```

8.
```
        2   9
        1   7
        3   0
+   9   9
```

9.
```
        5   8
        4   9
        7   3
+   2   8
```

10.
```
        8   3
        4   9
        2   9
+   1   8
```

11.
```
  €1 ·2  9
x        6
```

12.
```
  €4 ·1  2
x        9
```

13.
```
  €3 ·1  7
x        8
```

14.
```
  €6 ·6  5
x        7
```

15.
```
  €4 ·8  0
x        6
```

16. 6) 4 8 6

17. 8) 4 8 8

18. 9) 8 3 7

19. 7) 5 7 4

20. 9) 8 6 4

B Work it out.

1.
```
        5   6
x   1   6
```

2.
```
        7   1
x   2   8
```

3.
```
        4   9
x   3   7
```

4.
```
        7   2
x   4   6
```

5.
```
        6   2
x   4   5
```

6.
```
        2   1   6
+   3   8   8

-   2   9   9
```

7.
```
        4   1   3
+   2   6   5

-   3   6   6
```

8.
```
        5   3   7
+   2   8   4

-   4   1   6
```

9.
```
        5   2   8
+   3   1   7

-   4   2   8
```

10.
```
        7   1   2
+   1   8   8

-   5   6   7
```

11. 6) 5 0 7

12. 8) 4 9 0

13. 9) 8 9 3

14. 7) 8 8 6

15. 9) 9 3 7

16.
```
        3   6
x   4   5
```

17.
```
        2   8
x   1   7
```

18.
```
        4   6
x   3   3
```

19.
```
        5   6
x   2   7
```

20.
```
        5   8
x   3   7
```

A Figure it out.

> **Mrs Tabby loves cats. She has 18 cats! Mr Woof lives next door and loves dogs. What can you tell about them?**

1. $\frac{1}{3}$ of the cats are grey. How many cats are grey? ☐

2. $\frac{1}{3}$ of the other cats are marmalade. How many are marmalade? ☐

3. The other cats are black. How many cats are black? ☐

4. The cost of food for each cat is €2·00 a week. What is the total weekly cost? € ☐

5. Mrs Tabby buys 7 bags of cat treats a week at 90c a bag. How much is that? € ☐

6. How many legs altogether do the grey cats have? ☐

7. $\frac{1}{2}$ of all the grey cats wear bells. How many grey cats have bells? ☐

8. Mr Woof has half as many dogs as Mrs Tabby has cats. How many dogs? ☐

9. How many animals altogether do Mrs Tabby and Mr Woof have? ☐

10. How many ears altogether do Mr Woof's dogs have? ☐

B Think it out. Tick (✔) the correct answer.

1. 3 bags weigh 4·17 kg, 2·66 kg and 1·48 kg. What is the total weight?
   a 7·31 kg b 8·31 kg c 8·35 kg

2. The school has 4 teams of 15 children. How many children in total? a 19 b 30 c 60

3. A film begins at 3:15 p.m. and ends at 5:10 p.m. How long is that? a 1 hr 5 mins b 1 hr 25 mins c 1 hr 55 mins

4. Raffle tickets are 25c each or 5 for €1·00. How much for 13 tickets?
   a €2·75 b €3·25 c €5·25

5. How many 2c coins make up 50c?
   a 52 b 50 c 25

6. What is the perimeter of a triangle if its sides are 9 cm, 4 cm and 6 cm?
   a 9 cm b 12 cm c 19 cm

7. By how much is 32·7 less than 43·8?
   a 11·1 b 11·9 c 76·5

8. An €8·40 book was reduced by $\frac{1}{4}$. What is the new price? a €2·10 b €4·20 c €6·30

9. 7 children shared 63 sweets. How many did each get? a 9 b 8 c 7

10. What is missing? (5 x 6) − 4 ☐ (3 x 8) + 6
    a > b < c =

> If you need to, you can work out these sums in your copy.

C Puzzle it out. Do the sums and use the answers to crack the code.

G	544	R	612	D	810	E	675	S	663	F	564	O	792	I	429	A	726	N	936

1. 45 x 18 = ☐
2. 66 x 12 = ☐
3. 34 x 16 = ☐
4. 39 x 17 = ☐
5. 33 x 22 = ☐
6. 34 x 18 = ☐
7. 45 x 15 = ☐
8. 32 x 17 = ☐
9. 24 x 33 = ☐
10. 72 x 11 = ☐
11. 90 x 9 = ☐
12. 47 x 12 = ☐
13. 36 x 17 = ☐
14. 39 x 11 = ☐
15. 27 x 25 = ☐
16. 36 x 26 = ☐
17. 30 x 27 = ☐
18. 51 x 13 = ☐

Sum No.	1	2	3	4	5	6	7	8	9	10	11	12	13	14	15	16	17	18
Answer																		
Code																		

Unit 17 - Check-up

A Tables

1. 6 + ☐ = 14   4. ☐ − 7 = 8   7. 3 x ☐ = 24   10. 54 ÷ ☐ = 6

2. ☐ − 9 = 8   5. 8 x 7 = ☐   8. ☐ ÷ 6 = 8

3. 14 − ☐ = 5   6. ☐ x 6 = 36   9. ☐ ÷ 9 = 8

Score ☐

B Computation

1.		4	0	6
		3	1	5
	+	1	8	8

2.		6	0	8
	−			
		2	6	8

3.			7	3
		x	1	2

4.	€3	0	·4	4
	− €1	9	·7	6
	+ €4	5	·6	7

5.			5	9
		x	1	2
	3			

Give yourself 2 marks for each correct sum. **Score** ☐

C Fractions and Decimals

1. $\frac{9}{10}$ of 100 = ☐

2. $\frac{3}{4}$ of 8 = ☐

3. $\frac{1}{5}$ of 5·5 = ☐

4. 4·2 − 0·9 = ☐

5. 4·4 − 2 + 1·3 = ☐

6. 3·3 − 1·2 = ☐

7. 1·5 − 0·5 + 4 = ☐

8. 1·3 + 0·5 + 1·9 = ☐

9. $\frac{1}{6}$ of 18 less $\frac{1}{3}$ of 3 = ☐

10. $\frac{1}{3}$ of 9 plus $\frac{1}{2}$ of 8 = ☐

Score ☐

D Shapes, Measures and Data... Ring the number or amount that does not belong.

1. 2·5,   2·55, $2\frac{1}{2}$

2. 45 cm,   €0·45,   45c

3. 2·3 m,   23 cm,   0·23 m

4. 2 mins,   100 secs,   120 secs

5. 0·5 kg,   250 g,   0·25 kg

6. $\frac{1}{3}$, $\frac{2}{6}$, $\frac{3}{6}$

7. 0·5 m,   50 cm,   500 cm

8. 1·4 kg,   1400 g,   14 g

9. 150 secs,   1·5 mins,   90 secs

10. $\frac{6}{8}$, $\frac{8}{12}$, $\frac{3}{4}$

Score ☐

E Problem Solving... Tick (✓) the correct answer.

1. How many 4s in 31?   a ☐ 6   b ☐ 7   c ☐ 8

2. How many metres is 220 cm?   a ☐ 2 m   b ☐ 2·2 m   c ☐ 2·02 m

3. By how much is 9·1 greater than 7·2?   a ☐ 1·9   b ☐ 1·1   c ☐ 2·1

4. What is missing? 44 ÷ 4 ☐ 48 ÷ 4   a ☐ >   b ☐ =   c ☐ <

5. How much for 7 biros at 25c each?   a ☐ €1·45   b ☐ €1·65   c ☐ €1·75

Give yourself 2 marks for each correct answer. **Score** ☐

Unit 18 - Quick Questions

A Tables

1. 5 x $\boxed{10}$ = 50
4. $\boxed{9}$ x 4 = 36
7. 27 ÷ $\boxed{?}$ = 3
10. 60 ÷ $\boxed{5}$ = 12

2. $\boxed{7}$ x 11 = 77
5. 6 x $\boxed{7}$ = 42
8. $\boxed{84}$ ÷ 12 = 7
11. $\boxed{66}$ ÷ 11 = 6

3. 9 x $\boxed{5}$ = 45
6. 7 x $\boxed{7}$ = 49
9. 64 ÷ $\boxed{8}$ = 8
12. $\boxed{54}$ ÷ 6 = 9

B Calculate.

1. (9 x 6) + 8 = ☐
5. 357 – ☐ = 199
9. 605 ÷ 5 = ☐

2. (7 x 9) – 3 = ☐
6. 324 – ☐ = 164
10. 909 ÷ 9 = ☐

3. (9 x 8) – 2 = ☐
7. 5 x 7 x 2 = ☐
11. €2·67 – €☐ = €1·08

4. (7 x 4) + 5 = ☐
8. 5 x 8 ÷ 2 = ☐
12. €4·24 – €☐ = €3·04

C Numbers... Complete the sequences.

1. 57, 47, 37, ☐, ☐, ☐
7. 15, 18, 21, ☐, ☐, ☐

2. 6, 13, 20, ☐, ☐, ☐
8. 64, 56, 48, ☐, ☐, ☐

3. 16, 21, 26, ☐, ☐, ☐
9. 2·3, 3·4, 4·5, ☐, ☐, ☐

4. 8, 16, 24, ☐, ☐, ☐
10. 6·5, 7, 7·5, ☐, ☐, ☐

5. 17, 23, 29, ☐, ☐, ☐
11. 33, 45, 57, ☐, ☐, ☐

6. 49, 46, 43, ☐, ☐, ☐
12. 99, 87, 75, ☐, ☐, ☐

D Money... Find the cost of each shopping list.

 Bar (B) = 30c   Cone (C) = €1·00   Sweet (S) = 20c

1. 2B + 1C + 1S = €☐
7. 3B + 4C + 1S = €☐

2. 1B + 2C + 2S = €☐
8. 2B + 1C + 4S = €☐

3. 1B + 1C + 4S = €☐
9. 3B + 4C = €☐

4. 4B + 1C = €☐
10. 1B + 3C = €☐

5. 1B + 1C + 1S = €☐
11. 4C + 5S = €☐

6. 2B + 2C + 2S = €☐
12. 2B + 1C + 3S = €☐

E Figure it out. True (✓) or false (✗)?

1. 9 divides evenly into 56. ☐
7. A triangle is $\frac{1}{3}$ of a square. ☐

2. 49 is a multiple of 7. ☐
8. 1·25 is less than 1·5. ☐

3. $\frac{1}{5}$ of 205 is 41. ☐
9. 3·75 – 1·25 = 2·5 ☐

4. $\frac{1}{4}$ of 28 is 8. ☐
10. 309 < 319 ☐

5. 27 is half of 64. ☐
11. One-fifth of 100 is 10. ☐

6. 8·15 p.m. is evening time. ☐
12. €4·30 – €0·50 = €3·70 ☐

Be careful! Some division sums have remainders.

A Work it out.

1.	2 9 9 × 7	2.	5 1 8 × 6	3.	4 2 9 × 8	4.	3 2 9 × 6	5.	6 4 7 × 9

6.	6 9 × 4 8	7.	2 8 × 7 3	8.	9 4 × 4 5	9.	4 8 × 5 7	10.	7 5 × 2 9

11.	5 0 0 7 − 1 4 7 6	12.	2 1 2 5 − 8 7 6	13.	3 0 6 0 − 2 6 6 6	14.	2 5 4 6 − 1 8 8 6	15.	3 0 0 4 − 1 6 8 7

16.
```
      3 0
  2     6
+     4 5
  7 1 2
```

17.
```
    2     8
    3 5
+     4 4
  7 2 1
```

18.
```
  1 3 4
    4 5
+     0 6
  7 9 8
```

19.
```
      4 4
    3 4
+ 2     7
  7 5 6
```

20.
```
          2
        3 4
+ 3 9
  6 8 8
```

B Work it out.

1.
```
  1 8 7
  2 9 9
+ 2 7 6
```

2.
```
  2 7 8
  3 0 9
+ 2 4 7
```

3.
```
  4 2 5
  1 1 6
+ 3 8 2
```

4.
```
  8 7 3
  8 8 8
+ 5 4 9
```

5.
```
  7 3 2
  5 6 3
+ 9 3 4
```

6.
```
  €4·37
  €5·23
+ €2·24
```

7.
```
  €1·56
  €2·39
+ €2·62
```

8.
```
  €4·19
  €2·77
+ €2·19
```

9.
```
  €2·37
  €5·44
+ €1·28
```

10.
```
  €3·22
  €1·39
+ €5·67
```

11.	8) 5 6 3 R	12.	6) 7 6 4 R	13.	7) 6 0 8 R	14.	9) 9 3 4 R	15.	8) 6 1 2 R

16.	6 2 × 5 3	17.	4 7 × 5 6	18.	2 7 × 2 9	19.	1 8 × 5 4	20.	6 6 × 2 3

A Making Shapes: The Shape Village... Imagine you are building a shape village. Draw and colour your village using only regular shapes.

1. Library:
Use only rectangles and circles.

2. Church:
Use only rectangles and triangles.

3. Playground:
Use all 5 shapes.

4. Shop:
Use only squares, rectangles and ovals.

5. Some houses:
Use any shapes you like.

6. School:
Use all 5 shapes.

Unit 18 - Check-up

A Tables

1. ☐ + 9 = 16
2. ☐ + 9 = 17
3. 5 + ☐ = 15
4. 13 − 5 = ☐
5. 17 − ☐ = 8
6. ☐ − 10 = 3
7. 6 × 9 = ☐
8. ☐ × 8 = 72
9. 60 ÷ 6 = ☐
10. 45 ÷ ☐ = 5

Score ☐

B Computation

1.				2.	5	1	2	5	3.		m	cm	4.	€1	1	·4	4	5.		6	0	6
		4	2	7							4	0	0	−		€9	·3	7			+	1	9	9
	+	2	0	9		x		3			1	0	6							5			
		8	2	8						+	3	2	0		x			5				

Give yourself 2 marks for each correct sum. **Score** ☐

C Fractions and Decimals... Ring the correct amount.

1.	0·3	☺☺☺☺☺☺☺☺☺☺	6.	2/3	🏠🏠🏠🏠🏠🏠
2.	0·7	🚗🚗🚗🚗🚗🚗🚗🚗🚗🚗	7.	0·1	🎗🎗🎗🎗🎗🎗🎗🎗🎗🎗
3.	1/6	👂👂👂👂👂👂👂👂👂👂👂👂	8.	0·25	⛵⛵⛵⛵⛵⛵⛵⛵
4.	0·6	🚲🚲🚲🚲🚲🚲🚲🚲🚲🚲	9.	1/2	♥♥♥♥♥♥♥♥♥♥♥♥
5.	0·5	🚚🚚🚚🚚🚚🚚🚚🚚🚚🚚	10.	3/4	✦✦✦✦✦✦✦✦

Score ☐

D Shapes, Measures and Data

Answer the questions.

1. How many €0·60 apples can I buy with €2·50? ☐

2. If kiwis are 25c each or 5 for €1·00, how many kiwis will I get if I spend €2·50? ☐

Which measure is greater?

3. 500 g or 0·2 kg? ☐

4. 25 l or 250 ml? ☐

5. 100 g or 0·25 kg? ☐

Give yourself 2 marks for each correct answer. **Score** ☐

E Problem Solving

There are 28 pupils in 4th class. Half of them are 10 years old. One-quarter of them are 9 and the rest are 8. Half of the ten-year-olds are boys. In total, the class has two more boys than girls.

1. How many pupils are 10 years old? ☐
2. How many pupils are 9 years old? ☐
3. How many pupils are 8 years old? ☐
4. How many girls are 10 years old? ☐
5. How many boys in total are in the class? ☐

Give yourself 2 marks for each correct answer. **Score** ☐

Unit 19 - Quick Questions

A Tables

1. 9 + 10 = ☐
2. ☐ + 9 = 17
3. 14 – ☐ = 6
4. 16 – ☐ = 7
5. 9 + 8 = ☐
6. 9 x 7 = ☐
7. 5 x 8 = ☐
8. 4 x 12 = ☐
9. 63 ÷ 7 = ☐
10. 72 ÷ 8 = ☐
11. 56 ÷ ☐ = 7
12. 48 ÷ ☐ = 6

B Calculate.

1. 24 + 37 = ☐
2. 533 – 212 = ☐
3. 139 + 401 = ☐
4. 452 + 225 = ☐
5. 454 – 144 = ☐
6. 144 x 2 = ☐
7. 690 ÷ 6 = ☐
8. 135 + 114 + 100 = ☐
9. 246 + 122 + 101 = ☐
10. 212 + 103 + 113 = ☐
11. (5 x 6) – ☐ = 22
12. (4 x 7) – ☐ = 24

C Numbers... Are these numbers > (greater than), < (less than) or = (equal to) each other?

1. 30 ÷ 3 ☐ 12
2. 17 + 22 ☐ 31 + 10
3. 456 – 10 ☐ 406 + 10
4. 62 – 20 ☐ 42 + 20
5. (5 x 6) + 3 ☐ (3 x 10) + 5
6. 3 x 4 ☐ 10 + 4
7. 10 + 8 + 12 ☐ 11 + 4 + 11
8. 5·2 + 1·3 ☐ 3·4 + 3·3
9. 6 x 6 ☐ 5 x 7
10. 9·5 + 8·5 ☐ 18
11. 0·25 + 0·25 ☐ $\frac{1}{2}$
12. €3·50 – €1·20 ☐ €2·00 + €1·20

D Money... Write the totals as euros and cents.

1. 50c + 129c = €1·79
2. 226c + 103c = €☐
3. 135c + 345c = €☐
4. 29c + 207c = €☐
5. 33c + 199c = €☐
6. 318c + 80c = €☐
7. 69c + 156c = €☐
8. 448c + 60c = €☐
9. 384c – 62c = €☐
10. 109c – 50c = €☐
11. 244c – 140c = €☐
12. 526c – 260c = €☐

E Figure it out. Tick (✓) the correct answer.

1. 24 + 13 – 6 = a 29 b 31 c 33
2. 30 – 8 + 3 = a 22 b 25 c 41
3. (6 x 2) + 4 = a 12 b 14 c 16
4. (9 ÷ 3) x 2 = a 5 b 6 c 12
5. (3 x 5) – 7 = a 8 b 7 c 15
6. (36 ÷ 4) – 4 = a 2 b 3 c 5
7. (2·2 x 3) + 2 = a 6·8 b 8·6 c 8·8
8. $\frac{3}{4}$ of 20 = a 5 b 12 c 15
9. 4 m 70 cm =
   a 47 cm b 407 cm c 470 cm

10. €1·25 + €1·25 + €1·25 =
    a €3·50 b €3·60 c €3·75
11. (€2·99 – €2·59) x 5 =
    a €2·00 b €5·00 c €5·99
12. 1 m 23 cm + 2 m 04 cm =
    a 327 cm b 363 cm c 367 cm

A Work it out.

1.
```
    4  1  2
  x       7
```

2.
```
    3  3  2
  x       9
```

3.
```
    4  2  5
  x       8
```

4.
```
    2  0  6
  x       6
```

5.
```
    3  6  7
  x       5
```

6.
```
       2  4
    1  6
  +       5
    6  0  8
```

7.
```
    2     4
    4  1
  +    2  0
    7  8  8
```

8.
```
       2  1
    2     4
  +    1  5
    5  0  0
```

9.
```
    2     3
       5  4
  +       6
    7  2  0
```

10.
```
    1     2
    1  7
  +    1  7
    6  6  9
```

11.
```
  €4 ·2 6
  x      8
```

12.
```
  €7 ·7 7
  x      6
```

13.
```
  €6 ·8 3
  x      4
```

14.
```
  €5 ·7 8
  x      7
```

15.
```
  €7 ·5 5
  x      9
```

16. 4)€7·44
17. 9)€6·75
18. 7)€6·65
19. 6)€4·26
20. 8)€6·64

B Work it out.

1.
```
   m  cm
   1  8  0
   2  0  5
 + 6  3  0
```

2.
```
   m  cm
   2  0  7
   1  5  0
 + 2  3  4
```

3.
```
   m  cm
   1  4  0
   2  0  9
 + 1  6  8
```

4.
```
   m  cm
   2  4  0
   2  0  5
 + 1  8  0
```

5.
```
   m  cm
   2  6  5
   1  8  0
 + 2  2  5
```

6.
```
      3  4
  x   3  6
```

7.
```
      8  6
  x   7  5
```

8.
```
      3  9
  x   4  6
```

9.
```
      5  7
  x   8  9
```

10.
```
      7  3
  x   4  7
```

11.
```
      9  4
  x   7  6
```

12.
```
      3  8
  x   7  7
```

13.
```
      4  9
  x   5  3
```

14.
```
      4  7
  x   6  8
```

15.
```
      8  8
  x   2  7
```

16.
```
  €5 4 ·2 8
 -€2 7 ·1 9
```

17.
```
  €6 0 ·5 6
 -€5 4 ·9 9
```

18.
```
  €5 5 ·5 1
 -€3 6 ·6 0
```

19.
```
  €8 7 ·4 4
 -€7 6 ·2 7
```

20.
```
  €2 7 ·3 8
 -€1 9 ·6 3
```

Unit 19 - Problems

A Figure it out.

1. Drinks are 35c each or 3 for €1·00. How much for 10 drinks? € [ ]

2. A triangle has a 23 cm perimeter. 2 sides are 6 cm and 7 cm. The 3rd side is [ ] cm.

3. Jenny had €5. She spent €1·20, 90c and €1·30. How much has she left? € [ ]

4. Tom got $\frac{1}{4}$ of 16 marbles. Kim and Úna shared the rest. How many did Kim get? [ ]

5. 5 tickets cost €18. The 2 adult tickets cost €4·50 each. How much is a child's ticket? € [ ]

6. Three children jumped 1·2 m, 0·9 m and 1·7 m. What was the total of the jumps? [ ] m

7. Stamps are 60c each. How many stamps can you buy for €4·95? [ ]

8. A programme begins at 7:25 p.m. and ends at 8:10 p.m. How long is that? [ ] mins

9. Pat kept 12 of his 27 cars. He shared the rest among 3 friends. Each got [ ].

10. May is 2 years older than her twin sisters. Together their ages add to 14. What age is May?
[ ]

B Think it out. Tick (✓) the correct answer.

1. Joy read $\frac{3}{4}$ of a book with 160 pages. She read [ ] pages. a 40 b 80 c 120

2. Meat costs €2·50 per kg. How much for 200 g? a 50c b €1·25 c €5·00

3. A bus leaves at 6:40 a.m. and travels for 55 mins. It arrives at
a 6:95 a.m. b 7:15 a.m. c 7:35 a.m.

4. A rectangle is 5 cm wide and 12 cm long. What is the perimeter?
a 17 cm b 34 cm c 60 cm

5. How many 8s in 50? a 5 b 6 c 8

6. How many angles in a rectangle?
a 2 b 3 c 4

7. By how much is 406 less than 619?
a 213 b 225 c 1025

8. A box had 48 sweets. 12 were eaten. What fraction is that? a $\frac{1}{8}$ b $\frac{1}{4}$ c $\frac{1}{2}$

9. What is missing? 23 − 6 [ ] = 31 − 10 + 4
a + 8 b + 4 c − 8

10. Triplets weighed 2·8 kg, 2·4 kg and 1·9 kg. What was the total weight?
a 5·21 kg b 6·1 kg c 7·1 kg

C Puzzle it out. Use the 100-square to complete the tasks.

1. Ring every 11th number, starting with 11.

2. Write 5 multiples of 9. [ ], [ ], [ ], [ ], [ ]

3. What number is 46 less than 81? [ ]

4. Put a line though every 8th number, starting with 8.

5. Write 5 multiples of 12. [ ], [ ], [ ], [ ], [ ]

6. Start at 41 and count back 19 to [ ].

7. Put an x on any number that is a multiple of 6.

8. Write three numbers that divide evenly into 16.
[ ], [ ], [ ]

1	2	3	4	5	6	7	8	9	10
11	12	13	14	15	16	17	18	19	20
21	22	23	24	25	26	27	28	29	30
31	32	33	34	35	36	37	38	39	40
41	42	43	44	45	46	47	48	49	50
51	52	53	54	55	56	57	58	59	60
61	62	63	64	65	66	67	68	69	70
71	72	73	74	75	76	77	78	79	80
81	82	83	84	85	86	87	88	89	90
91	92	93	94	95	96	97	98	99	100

Unit 19 - Check-up

A Tables

1. $7 + 9 = \boxed{}$ 4. $\boxed{} - 7 = 8$ 7. $\boxed{} \times 7 = 56$ 10. $56 \div \boxed{} = 7$

2. $27 \div \boxed{} = 3$ 5. $\boxed{} + 9 = 19$ 8. $\boxed{} \div 7 = 6$

3. $4 + \boxed{} = 13$ 6. $\boxed{} \div 9 = 7$ 9. $8 \times 9 = \boxed{}$

Score $\boxed{}$

B Computation

1.		4	0	6		2.			3	9		3.			6	5		4.	€2	9	·0	4		5.		2	0	1
	−	3	8	5			x			8				3		0			€4	1	·9	9				1	8	9
												+		1	4		+	€1	5	·0	6		+	3	7	4	8
													7	9	4												

Give yourself 2 marks for each correct sum.   Score $\boxed{}$

C Fractions and Decimals... Tick (✓) the correct answer.

1. $4 - 2 \cdot 5 =$ a $1 \cdot 5$ b $2 \cdot 5$ c $6 \cdot 5$ 6. $2 \cdot 3 + 1 + 1 \cdot 2 =$ a $3 \cdot 5$ b 4 c $4 \cdot 5$

2. $1 \cdot 6 + 0 \cdot 3 =$ a $1 \cdot 3$ b $1 \cdot 6$ c $1 \cdot 9$ 7. $1 \cdot 2 + 1 \cdot 7 - 0 \cdot 4 =$ a $2\frac{1}{2}$ b $3\frac{1}{4}$ c $3\frac{1}{2}$

3. $\frac{1}{5}$ of $15 =$ a 3 b 5 c 18 8. $2 \cdot 5 - 1 \cdot 2 + 0 \cdot 6 =$ a $\frac{1}{2}$ b $1\frac{9}{10}$ c $2\frac{1}{2}$

4. $\frac{1}{5}$ of $100 =$ a 5 b 20 c 120 9. $4 \cdot 6 + 0 \cdot 5 + 1 \cdot 4 =$ a $3 \cdot 7$ b $4 \cdot 9$ c $6 \cdot 5$

5. $\frac{1}{8}$ of $16 =$ a 2 b 4 c 8 10. $\frac{1}{10}$ of $16 =$ a $1 \cdot 6$ b $2 \cdot 6$ c 26

Score $\boxed{}$

D Shapes, Measures and Data... Write the digital times.

1.    2.    3.    4.    5.

$\boxed{\quad : \quad}$ $\boxed{\quad : \quad}$ $\boxed{\quad : \quad}$ $\boxed{\quad : \quad}$ $\boxed{\quad : \quad}$

Give yourself 2 marks for each correct answer.   Score $\boxed{}$

E Problem Solving

1. Jim, Mel and Tom ran a race. Their total time was 1 hr 13 mins. Jim's time was 28 minutes, and Mel's was 22 minutes. What was Tom's time? $\boxed{}$ mins

2. Pat shared 22 sweets with 3 friends. He got 2 sweets more than his friends. How many sweets did each of his friends get? $\boxed{}$

3. A garage sold 24 cars. $\frac{1}{8}$ of the cars were red. How many red cars were sold? $\boxed{}$

4. Yoghurts are 25c each or 5 for €1·00. How much for 17? €$\boxed{}$

5. A shop sold €36·40 of goods. Children spent $\frac{1}{4}$ of this money. That is €$\boxed{}$.

Give yourself 2 marks for each correct answer.   Score $\boxed{}$

A Tables

1. 7 x ☐ = 56
2. ☐ x 5 = 45
3. 10 x ☐ = 70
4. ☐ x 8 = 56
5. 8 x ☐ = 72
6. 9 x ☐ = 81
7. 54 ÷ ☐ = 9
8. ☐ ÷ 10 = 4
9. 64 ÷ ☐ = 8
10. 24 ÷ ☐ = 3
11. ☐ x 8 = 72
12. ☐ ÷ 9 = 9

B Calculate.

1. 1723 + 147 = ☐
2. 2533 − 243 = ☐
3. 2458 + 1320 = ☐
4. 4140 + 1360 = ☐
5. 1656 − 1145 = ☐
6. 25 x 5 = ☐
7. 7·80 ÷ 4 = ☐
8. €3·42 + €2·57 = €☐
9. 3 + 7 − 0·5 = ☐
10. 4 − 0·5 + 3·5 = ☐
11. 2·25 + 2·25 = ☐
12. 5 + 1 − ☐ = 5·5

C Numbers... Ring the even numbers.

> Even numbers end in 0, 2, 4, 6 or 8.

1. ② 3 ④ 5 ⑥ 7 ⑧
2. 23 51 65 40 32 41 62
3. 32 39 35 34 38 37 31
4. 48 40 44 46 43 47 49
5. 101 98 96 89 83 80 78
6. 67 69 64 60 65 61 66
7. 153 136 123 145 128 143 129
8. 79 98 65 84 36 54 55
9. 25 16 32 21 18 11 12
10. 63 58 66 46 59 54 45
11. 106 113 142 145 126 147 138
12. 24 33 41 53 66 74 82

D Fractions

1. $\frac{1}{2}$ of 6 plus $\frac{1}{3}$ of 6 = ☐
2. $\frac{1}{3}$ of 9 plus $\frac{1}{3}$ of 6 = ☐
3. $\frac{1}{4}$ of 20 plus $\frac{1}{2}$ of 24 = ☐
4. $\frac{1}{4}$ of 12 plus $\frac{1}{2}$ of 6 = ☐
5. $\frac{1}{4}$ of 8 plus $\frac{1}{4}$ of 12 = ☐
6. $\frac{1}{2}$ of 18 plus $\frac{1}{4}$ of 16 = ☐
7. $\frac{1}{2}$ of 30 plus $\frac{1}{4}$ of 8 = ☐
8. $\frac{1}{4}$ of 16 plus $\frac{1}{4}$ of 8 = ☐
9. $\frac{1}{4}$ of 8 less $\frac{1}{4}$ of 4 = ☐
10. $\frac{1}{4}$ of 44 less $\frac{1}{4}$ of 4 = ☐
11. $\frac{1}{3}$ of 99 = ☐
12. $\frac{2}{3}$ of 99 = ☐

E Figure it out. Use + , − , X or ÷ to complete the number sentences.

1. 18 ☐ 9 ☐ 4 = 13
2. (4 ☐ 5) ☐ 5 = 25
3. (21 ☐ 3) ☐ 2 = 5
4. (16 ☐ 4) ☐ 1 = 5
5. (€2·50 ☐ 2) ☐ €3·00 = €8·00
6. (€1·50 ☐ 3) ☐ €0·50 = €4·00
7. (6 ☐ 2) ☐ 9 = 72
8. 2·5 ☐ 2·5 ☐ 1 = 4
9. (9 ☐ 3) ☐ 4 = 12
10. 28 ☐ 12 ☐ 16 = 24
11. 6·6 ☐ 2 ☐ 5 = 9·6
12. (32 ☐ 4) ☐ 5 = 40

A Work it out.

1. 8 | 784
2. 5 | 600
3. 9 | 396
4. 7 | 273
5. 6 | 378

6.
```
    3 2
x   4 5
```

7.
```
    2 9
x   2 7
```

8.
```
    3 5
x   4 9
```

9.
```
    2 6
x   3 4
```

10.
```
    2 4
x   3 6
```

11.
```
    3 7 4
-     2 9
    1 5 5
```

12.
```
      3 2
-     1 9
    1 3 9
```

13.
```
    6     2
-       0
    4 0 0
```

14.
```
   m  cm
   3  6 0
   1  2 7
+  2  3 5
```

15.
```
   m  cm
   2  4 8
   1  7 0
+  1  0 4
```

16.
```
    6 0 2
-   2 3 5
```

17.
```
    7 1 2
-   3 7 7
```

18.
```
    7 2 2
-   2 4 3
```

19.
```
    6 9 7
-   2 3 4
```

20.
```
    6 5 4
-   2 3 3
```

B Work it out.

1.
```
  €3 7 ·3 0
- €2 7 ·0 7
```

2.
```
  €5 6 ·2 9
- €2 4 ·3 8
```

3.
```
  €7 6 ·5 0
- €3 6 ·6 4
```

4.
```
  €6 0 ·4 5
- €2 6 ·5 6
```

5.
```
  €8 3 ·2 9
- €3 5 ·3 1
```

6. 7 | €4.55
7. 4 | €4.92
8. 6 | €6.48
9. 9 | €6.39
10. 9 | €9.63

11.
```
  €7 ·8 7
x       9
```

12.
```
  €8 ·7 9
x       8
```

13.
```
  €4 ·7 3
x       7
```

14.
```
  €9 ·2 8
x       6
```

15.
```
  €7 ·8 8
x       9
```

16.
```
    3 7
x   2 9
```

17.
```
    8 4
x   3 8
```

18.
```
    5 9
x   4 3
```

19.
```
    2 7
x   1 4
```

20.
```
    6 8
x   3 9
```

21.
```
    8 3 8
-   2 6 7
```

22.
```
    6 9 3
-   2 0 0
```

23.
```
    6 5 6
-   2 2 8
```

24.
```
    6 1 6
-   2 4 4
```

25.
```
    6 0 6
-   2 4 4
```

(handwritten: 80 +6 / 0 / 0)

A Figure it out.

Daffodils: 40c	Tulips: 30c	Daisies: 25c	Roses: 60c	Foxgloves: 50c	Poppies: 35c

Jane works in a flower shop. On Friday she has a special offer: *Buy 6 flowers for the price of 5!*

1. What 3 **different** flowers could you buy for exactly €1·50? *Daffo, Roses, Forglo*

2. What 3 **different** flowers could you buy for exactly €1·00? *Daffo, Poppi, Dai~*

3. Nora bought 2 daffodils, 1 poppy and 3 foxgloves on Thursday. How much? € *2.80*

4. Tom bought 6 roses on Tuesday. How much? € *9.60*

5. How many tulips could Tom buy for what he paid for the roses? *10*

6. How much would Tom save if he bought the roses on Friday? €

7. On Friday, Jane bought 6 tulips and 6 daffodils. How much? €

8. Harry spent €7·00 on poppies on Monday. How many did he buy?

(handwritten working: 60 30 / x6 +9 / 360 270 / 600 030 / 960.00)

B Think it out. Tick (✓) the correct answer.

1. Four thousand and sixty-nine =
   a 4069   b 4690   c 4960

2. How much for 7 litres of milk at €1·25 a litre?   a €7·95   b €8·25   c €8·75

3. A journey starts at 6:35 p.m. and takes 50 mins. When does it end?
   a 6:25 p.m.   b 7:25 p.m.   c 7:55 p.m.

4. How many 9s in 59?   a 5   b 6   c 7

5. By how much is 409 greater than 348?
   a 52   b 59   c 61

6. What is $\frac{1}{3}$ of 15 plus $\frac{1}{4}$ of 20?   a 8   b 9   c 10

7. 34 − 17 ___ (3 x 4) + 5   a >   b <   c =

8. 14 chairs are in a room. That is a total of ___ chair legs.   a 18   b 48   c 56

C Puzzle it out. Do the sums and complete the cross-number puzzle.

Across
1. 29 x 16 =
3. 19 x 15 =
6. 111 x 5 =
8. 999 − 62 =
10. 101 x 7 =
11. 13 x 3 =
13. 8 x 7 =
15. 152 x 4 =
17. 63 x 3 =
19. 122 x 6 =
20. 9 x 7 =

Down
1. 2013 + 2112 =
2. 7 x 7 =
3. 81 ÷ 3 =
4. 7000 − 1257 =
5. 2045 + 1681 =
7. 217 + 316 =
9. 600 − 282 =
12. 4067 + 4969 =
14. 1198 + 4814 =
16. 203 x 4 =
18. 12 x 8 =
19. 12 x 6 =

If you need to, you can work out these sums in your copy.

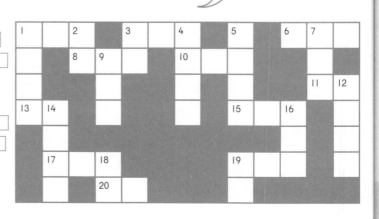

82

Unit 20 - Check-up

A Tables

1. $8 + \boxed{} = 17$ 4. $\boxed{} - 8 = 6$ 7. $\boxed{} \times 3 = 27$ 10. $56 \div \boxed{} = 8$

2. $\boxed{} - 8 = 7$ 5. $8 \times 6 = \boxed{}$ 8. $\boxed{} \div 8 = 6$

3. $13 - \boxed{} = 6$ 6. $\boxed{} \times 6 = 54$ 9. $\boxed{} \div 9 = 8$

Score $\boxed{}$

B Computation

1.		4	0	8	2.			8	3.			4	5	4.	€3	7	·5	6	5.			5	6
		3	8	8		−	5	6		×	2	3		+	€4	9	·2	6		×			9
	+	7	9	6		2	7	7															
														−	€2	0	·0	9		−	1	8	4

Give yourself 2 marks for each correct sum.

Score $\boxed{}$

C Fractions and Decimals

1. $0·8$ of $10 = \boxed{}$

2. $0·5$ of $6·4 = \boxed{}$

3. $\frac{2}{5}$ of $10 = \boxed{}$

4. $2·9 + 2·4 = \boxed{}$

5. $3·4 + 1·2 + 0·1 = \boxed{}$

3·3

6. $2·5 − 1·4 + 2 = \boxed{}$

7. $3·3 + 1·3 − 1 = \boxed{}$

8. $4·7 − 1·5 + 1·3 = \boxed{}$

9. $\frac{1}{5}$ of 20 plus $\frac{1}{2}$ of $4 = \boxed{}$

10. $\frac{1}{3}$ of 9 less $\frac{1}{2}$ of $4 = \boxed{}$

$\frac{1}{7}$

Score $\boxed{}$

D Shapes, Measures and Data

What measure is used (500 ml, 500 m or 500 g) to measure:

1.  $\boxed{}$ 2. $\boxed{}$ 3. $\boxed{}$

How much change will I have from €7·50 if I spend:

4. €3·20 and €1·90? € $\boxed{}$ 5. €5·03 and €0·99? € $\boxed{}$

Give yourself 2 marks for each correct answer.

Score $\boxed{}$

E Problem Solving... Tick (✓) the correct answer.

1. How many 5s in 43?   a 6   b 7   c 8

2. How many faces on a cube?   a 1   b 4   c 6

3. By how much is 3·9 less than 5?   a 0·1   b 1·1   c 1·4

4. What is missing? $72 \div 12$ ▊ $49 \div 7$ a >   b =   c <

5. How much for 7 biros at 81c each?   a €5·47   b €5·67   c €6·37

Give yourself 2 marks for each correct answer.

Score $\boxed{}$

Unit 21 - Quick Questions

A Tables

1. 6 + 12 = ☐
2. 5 + 8 = ☐
3. 11 – 5 = ☐
4. 17 – ☐ = 8
5. ☐ + 12 = 15
6. ☐ x 7 = 63
7. 9 x ☐ = 54
8. 4 x ☐ = 48
9. 21 ÷ ☐ = 7
10. 50 ÷ ☐ = 10
11. ☐ ÷ 9 = 5
12. 36 ÷ ☐ = 6

B Calculate.

1. 17 + ☐ = 52
2. 26 + ☐ = 41
3. 14 + ☐ = 32
4. 44 – ☐ = 27
5. 31 – ☐ = 18
6. 51 – ☐ = 30
7. (4 x 7) – 2 = ☐
8. (6 x 8) – 7 = ☐
9. (45 ÷ 3) + 5 = ☐
10. (48 ÷ 4) – 6 = ☐
11. 3·25 + ☐ = 10
12. 10 – 4·25 = ☐

C Numbers... Complete the sequences.

1. 26, 29, 32, ☐, ☐, ☐
2. 13, 18, 23, ☐, ☐, ☐
3. 48, 42, 36, ☐, ☐, ☐
4. 7, 14, 21, ☐, ☐, ☐
5. 44, 40, 36, ☐, ☐, ☐
6. 15, 12, 9, ☐, ☐, ☐
7. 7, 9, 11, ☐, ☐, ☐
8. 45, 40, 35, ☐, ☐, ☐
9. 5·5, 6, 6·5, ☐, ☐, ☐
10. 2·25, 3·35, 4·45, ☐, ☐, ☐
11. 6·0, 5·8, 5·6, ☐, ☐, ☐
12. 3·4, 3·6, 3·8, ☐, ☐, ☐

D Time... In a marathon, John finished at 3:15. Write the time that each of the following finished:

	Athlete		Finished at		Athlete		Finished at
1.	John	—	3:15	7.	Luke	55 minutes later	
2.	Pat	15 minutes later	3:30	8.	Jack	35 minutes earlier	
3.	Eva	10 minutes earlier	3:05	9.	Tess	20 minutes earlier	
4.	Oscar	30 minutes later		10.	Shay	50 minutes later	
5.	Jill	5 minutes later		11.	Sophie	45 minutes later	
6.	Bobby	25 minutes earlier		12.	Bob	40 minutes later	

E Figure it out. True (✓) or false (✗)?

1. 77 is a multiple of 11. ☐
2. $\frac{1}{4}$ of 90 is 30. ☐
3. 35 is one-third of 99. ☐
4. 4·3 is half of 86. ☐
5. €2·43 + €3·25 = €3·86 ☐
6. €5·30 – €2·50 = €2·80 ☐
7. $\frac{1}{2}$ is the same as 0·5. ☐
8. 1·5 + 1·25 = 2·75 ☐
9. 37 + 43 > 8 x 10 ☐
10. One-third of 9 is 3. ☐
11. €5·05 – €0·50 = €4·55 ☐
12. 19 is half of 28. ☐

Be careful! Some division sums have remainders.

A Work it out.

1.	2.	3.	4.	5.
3 6 3 + 1 6 6	2 8 7 + 1 8 8	4 7 3 + 3 8 8	2 7 7 + 3 2 6	4 9 7 + 3 6 7

6.	7.	8.	9.	10.
4 _ 7 + 1 5 6 3 8	3 _ 0 + 2 0 5 8 5	3 _ 9 + _ 3 7 1 6	3 _ 6 + 2 4 6 1 9	2 _ 6 + _ 7 8 2 7

11.	12.	13.	14.	15.
4 3 6 4 7 7 + 1 3 2	8 2 3 4 6 5 + 1 7 8	6 0 2 1 6 6 + 2 0 6	3 7 7 1 2 8 + 2 3 4	5 1 2 1 9 1 + 1 5 9

16.	17.	18.	19.	20.
4 8 6 x _ 4	5 2 6 x _ 9	5 0 _ x 4 6	_ 4 0 x 3 5	_ 3 0 x 1 7

B Work it out.

1.	2.	3.	4.	5.
7) 4 0 7 R	9) 6 5 6 R	8) 4 8 8	6) 8 1 2 R	7) 4 0 6

6.	7.	8.	9.	10.
€2 4 ·3 8 + €3 3 ·4 1 − €2 5 ·6 6	€3 2 ·4 5 + €2 6 ·6 7 − €2 9 ·0 4	€4 3 ·5 5 + €1 9 ·3 8 − €2 8 ·9 5	€3 7 ·5 4 + €1 7 ·6 3 − €1 9 ·8 8	€2 5 ·7 0 + €3 4 ·9 2 − €1 7 ·6 7

11.	12.	13.	14.	15.
6 7 x 3 3	4 9 x 5 2	4 8 x 2 6	7 9 x 3 7	5 6 x 4 6

16.	17.	18.	19.	20.
7) 6 0 5 R	7) 8 2 8 R	7) 7 5 5 R	7) 6 4 4	7) 5 6 3 R

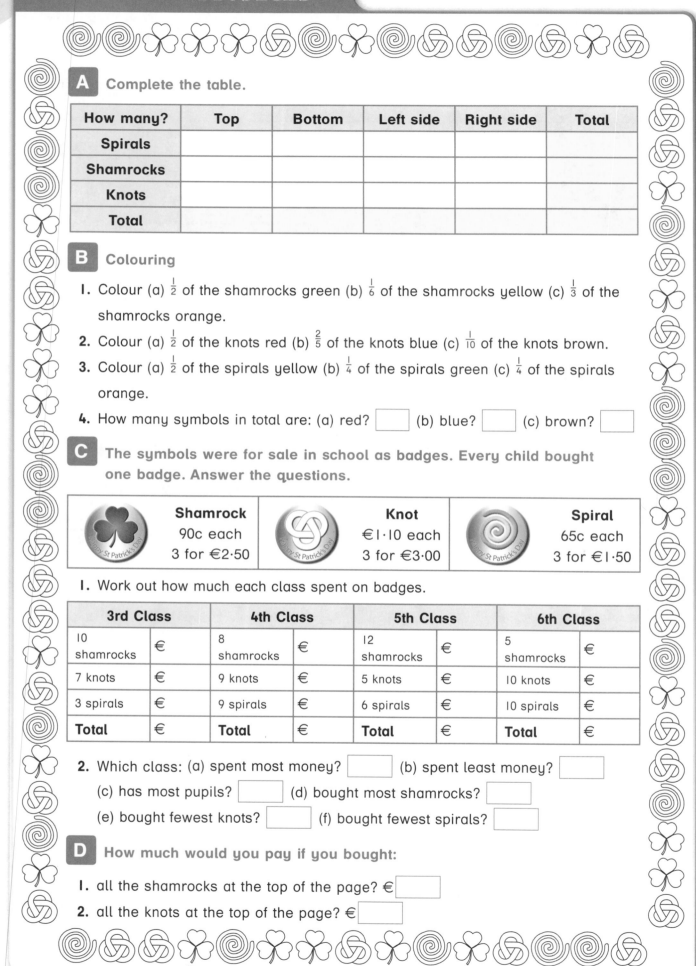

A Complete the table.

How many?	Top	Bottom	Left side	Right side	Total
Spirals					
Shamrocks					
Knots					
Total					

B Colouring

1. Colour (a) $\frac{1}{2}$ of the shamrocks green (b) $\frac{1}{6}$ of the shamrocks yellow (c) $\frac{1}{3}$ of the shamrocks orange.

2. Colour (a) $\frac{1}{2}$ of the knots red (b) $\frac{2}{5}$ of the knots blue (c) $\frac{1}{10}$ of the knots brown.

3. Colour (a) $\frac{1}{2}$ of the spirals yellow (b) $\frac{1}{4}$ of the spirals green (c) $\frac{1}{4}$ of the spirals orange.

4. How many symbols in total are: (a) red? ☐ (b) blue? ☐ (c) brown? ☐

C The symbols were for sale in school as badges. Every child bought one badge. Answer the questions.

Shamrock 90c each 3 for €2·50	Knot €1·10 each 3 for €3·00	Spiral 65c each 3 for €1·50

1. Work out how much each class spent on badges.

3rd Class		4th Class		5th Class		6th Class	
10 shamrocks	€	8 shamrocks	€	12 shamrocks	€	5 shamrocks	€
7 knots	€	9 knots	€	5 knots	€	10 knots	€
3 spirals	€	9 spirals	€	6 spirals	€	10 spirals	€
Total	€	Total	€	Total	€	Total	€

2. Which class: (a) spent most money? ☐ (b) spent least money? ☐

(c) has most pupils? ☐ (d) bought most shamrocks? ☐

(e) bought fewest knots? ☐ (f) bought fewest spirals? ☐

D How much would you pay if you bought:

1. all the shamrocks at the top of the page? € ☐

2. all the knots at the top of the page? € ☐

★ **Score each exercise out of 10.**

Unit 21 - Check-up

A Tables

1. 9 x 6 = ☐   4. 14 − 5 = ☐   7. 36 ÷ ☐ = 12   10. 84 ÷ 12 = ☐

2. 8 x 7 = ☐   5. 20 − ☐ = 10   8. ☐ ÷ 11 = 6

3. 5 x 7 = ☐   6. ☐ − 7 = 9   9. ☐ ÷ 5 = 8

Score ☐

B Computation

1.
```
        2
    1 0 8
  + 2   5
    9 7 4
```

2.
```
6 | 3 6 6
    x   7
```

3.
```
  m   cm
  5 2 7
  1 3 0
+ 2 0 6
```

4.
```
€1 0 · 4 0
− €5 · 5 4
```

5.
```
    5 2 0
  + 1 7 6
  4
```
x 8

Give yourself 2 marks for each correct sum. **Score** ☐

C Fractions and Decimals… Choose a correct answer from the list for each question.

2·5   2·6   4 $\frac{7}{10}$ 1·5   0·5   2·9   1   3·5   1·2

1. $3 - \frac{1}{4} + 1\frac{1}{4} =$ ☐

2. 5 − 3·5 = ☐

3. 1·5 + 1·4 = ☐

4. 1 − 0·5 = ☐

5. 1 + 0·2 + 1·3 = ☐

6. 2·4 − 1·2 = ☐

7. 1 − 0·5 + 0·5 = ☐

8. $\frac{3}{10} + \frac{4}{10} =$ ☐

9. 3 + 0·2 + 0·3 = ☐

10. 1·3 + 1·3 = ☐

Score ☐

D Shapes, Measures and Data

Ring the correct measure.

1. height: g   or   cm
2. weight: g   or   l
3. capacity: l   or   g

I had €8·00 but I only have €3·70 left.

How much did I spend?

4. €2·40 and € ☐

5. €1·90 and € ☐

Give yourself 2 marks for each correct answer. **Score** ☐

E Problem Solving

A train had 3 carriages and 60 passengers. $\frac{1}{3}$ of the passengers were in carriage A. $\frac{1}{2}$ were in carriage B and the others were in carriage C. $\frac{1}{10}$ of all the passengers bought a cup of tea on the train. The tea cost €2·20 each.

1. How many passengers were in carriage A? ☐

2. How many passengers were in carriage B? ☐

3. How many passengers were in carriage C? ☐

4. How many passengers bought a cup of tea? ☐

5. How much in total did the tea cost? € ☐

Give yourself 2 marks for each correct answer. **Score** ☐

87

Unit 22 - Quick Questions

A Tables

1. 8 x ☐ = 64
2. ☐ x 12 = 96
3. 7 x ☐ = 49
4. ☐ x 6 = 42
5. 5 x ☐ = 35
6. 8 x ☐ = 64
7. 49 ÷ ☐ = 7
8. ☐ ÷ 8 = 9
9. 48 ÷ ☐ = 8
10. 64 ÷ ☐ = 8
11. ☐ ÷ 6 = 7
12. ☐ ÷ 7 = 6

B Calculate.

1. 51 + 23 + 34 = ☐
2. 106 − ☐ = 88
3. 38 + 39 + 10 = ☐
4. 234 − 28 + 2 = ☐
5. 26 + 17 + 18 = ☐
6. 67 + 102 + 30 = ☐
7. 344 − 309 = ☐
8. (11 x 8) − 17 = ☐
9. (36 ÷ 6) + 14 = ☐
10. 49 + 29 + 21 = ☐
11. 132 + 10 − 15 = ☐
12. 9·63 − 4·51 = ☐

C Numbers... Write the largest number or amount.

1. 212, 112, 121, 211 ☐
2. 554, 544, 545, 455 ☐
3. 867, 786, 768, 876 ☐
4. 533, 534, 543, 544 ☐
5. €2·99, €2·79, €2·97, €2·90 € ☐
6. €7·44, €7·41, €7·14, €7·94 € ☐
7. €1·01, €1·09, €1·11, €1·19 € ☐
8. €4·23, €3·42, €4·33, €3·99 € ☐
9. $\frac{1}{10}$, $\frac{1}{4}$, $\frac{1}{2}$, $\frac{1}{3}$ ☐
10. $\frac{1}{4}$, $\frac{3}{4}$, $\frac{1}{2}$, $\frac{1}{6}$ ☐
11. 5·05, 5·11, 5·15, 5·51 ☐
12. 4·33, 4·13, 4·03, 4·23 ☐

D Fractions

1. one-third of 15 = ☐
2. two-thirds of 15 = ☐
3. one-quarter of 80 = ☐
4. half of 80 = ☐
5. three-quarters of 80 = ☐
6. half of 224 = ☐
7. one-tenth of 30 = ☐
8. one-quarter of 48 = ☐
9. one-third of 33 = ☐
10. two-thirds of 33 = ☐
11. four-tenths of 100 = ☐
12. six-tenths of 100 = ☐

E Figure it out. Tick (✓) the correct answer.

1. 33 + 66 + 1 = | a 99 | b 100 | c 101
2. 31 − 5 + 4 = | a 40 | b 35 | c 30
3. 34 + 36 + 25 = | a 95 | b 98 | c 105
4. $\frac{1}{4}$ of 24 = | a 4 | b 5 | c 6
5. (30 ÷ 5) x 2 = | a 10 | b 12 | c 14
6. 69 + 10 − 5 = | a 74 | b 79 | c 84
7. (21 ÷ 3) x 2 = | a 7 | b 14 | c 21
8. (19 − 14) x 2 = | a 7 | b 10 | c 30
9. (45 x 2) − 10 = | a 70 | b 80 | c 90
10. (33 − 6) + 13 = | a 26 | b 40 | c 52
11. (2·3 x 3) + 1·2 = | a 7·9 | b 8·0 | c 8·1
12. €4·69 − €2·55 = | a €2·14 | b €2·24 | c €2·44

(19 −14) x 2 =
34 + 36 + 25 =
(21 ÷ 3) x 2 =

A Work it out.

1.		4 5	2.		6 4	3.		3 6	4.		2 7	5.		8 9
	x	1 9		x	2 5		x	3 7		x	4 6		x	3 5

6.		4 2 6	7.		4 2 6	8.		1 8 7	9.		4 7 6	10.		3 1 7
		2 1 3			1 1 1			2 5 6			5 3 4			2 8 8
	+	6 2 2		+	5 2 4		+	2 2 2		+	2 0 1		+	4 0 1

11.	€2 ·3 3	12.	€2 2 ·1 1	13.	€2 5 ·2 3	14.	€1 3 ·2 2	15.	€1 7 ·3 7
	€1 5 ·2 2		€1 4 ·2 3		€4 4 ·4 4		€2 6 ·0 5		€4 7 ·2 9
+	€4 3 ·5 1	+	€3 4 ·7 7	+	€1 8 ·1 2	+	€2 7 ·1 4	+	€2 5 ·6 6

16.		4 5 7	17.		3 6 2	18.	2 8 7 3	19.	6 3 5 7	20.	3 0 2 7
	−	7 4		−	5 4	−	1 4 4 2	−	2 6 4	−	2 1 1 9

B Work it out.

1.	9 4 0 5	2.	7 6 7 9	3.	8 4 0 8	4.	9 7 2 0	5.	6 4 5 6

6.	hrs mins	7.	hrs mins	8.	hrs mins	9.	hrs mins	10.	hrs mins
	1 4 0		2 1 5		3 1 0		3 0 5		2 5 0
+	2 2 5	+	1 5 0	+	1 2 5	+	1 5 5	+	1 2 5
	4 0 5								

11.		2 4	12.		3 7	13.		3 5	14.		6 5	15.		4 9
	x	1 9		x	2 4		x	2 3		x	4 7		x	3 9

16.		7 7	17.		6 8	18.		4 9	19.		5 7	20.		7 4
	x	2 3		x	2 7		x	3 6		x	2 5		x	2 6

Unit 22 - Problems

A Figure it out.

1. Sam spent €7·80 in the shop. How much change from €10·00? € [   ]
2. There are 32 children in 4th class. 13 are boys. How many are girls? [   ]
3. One side of a square is 6 cm. What is the length of the perimeter? [   ] cm
4. There are 4 cars outside the school. How many wheels on all the cars? [   ]
5. A farmer has 12 cows, 23 sheep and 16 calves. How many animals altogether? [   ]
6. There are 3 boxes of 6 eggs in the fridge. How many eggs is that? [   ]
7. John goes to bed at 8:30 p.m., 10 mins before Jane. What is Jane's bedtime? [   ] p.m.
8. 3 pieces of string are 12 cm, 8 cm and 9 cm long. What length is that altogether? [   ] cm
9. Molly had €1·60. How many 50c ice-creams can she buy? [   ]
10. Twins and their 1-year-old sister have a total age of 9. What age are the twins? [   ]

B Think it out. Tick (✓) the correct answer.

1. 3 bags weigh 5·42 kg, 2·33 kg and 1·17 kg. What is the total weight?
   [a] 7·85 kg [b] 7·92 kg [c] 8·92 kg

2. $\frac{1}{3}$ of the 54 pupils in a school are absent. How many are present? [a] 18 [b] 36 [c] 51

3. A programme begins at 6:40 p.m. and ends at 7:30 p.m. How long is it?
   [a] 50 mins [b] 30 mins [c] 90 mins

4. Cans were 90c each or 6 for €5·00. How much for 14 cans?
   [a] €11·80 [b] €12·60 [c] €13·60

5. 7 oranges were each divided into 8 segments. How many segments?
   [a] 15 [b] 48 [c] 56

6. The perimeter of a square is 36 cm. What is the length of one side?
   [a] 4 cm [b] 9 cm [c] 12 cm

7. By how much is 70·6 greater than 64·5?
   [a] 5·1 [b] 6·1 [c] 7·1

8. An €86·40 dress was reduced by $\frac{1}{2}$. What is the new price?
   [a] €36·20 [b] €43·20 [c] €43·40

9. (3 x 7) + 10 [   ] (5 x 5) + 6
   [a] > [b] < [c] =

10. 5 children are aged 7, 11, 12, 13 and 16. What is the total of their ages?
    [a] 47 [b] 59 [c] 61

C Puzzle it out. Complete the Sudokus using 1, 2, 3, 4, 5 and 6 in each row and column.

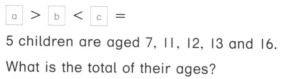

Remember! Use each number only once in each row and column.

1.

5	3	4			
			3	5	4
			2		
1		2			
			6	3	5
3	6	5			

2.

4		2		1	3
5		1		3	
	4		1		2
	1		3		6
1		4		6	
6		3		2	

Unit 22 - Check-up

A Tables

1. $4 + 9 = \boxed{}$ 4. $\boxed{} - 7 = 12$ 7. $4 \times \boxed{} = 48$ 10. $42 \div \boxed{} = 7$

2. $70 \div \boxed{} = 7$ 5. $16 - \boxed{} = 7$ 8. $56 \div 7 = \boxed{}$

3. $9 + \boxed{} = 17$ 6. $\boxed{} \div 9 = 6$ 9. $\boxed{} \times 9 = 81$

Score $\boxed{}$

B Computation

1.			2		2.		6	5	3.		2	8	5	4. €2	8	·0	5	5.		4	6	8
	−	3	8		×			9			1	6	8	€3	7	·8	6		+	2	9	5
		6	9						+			4	9	+ €1	9	·4	7					
																			−	3	6	7

Give yourself 2 marks for each correct sum.

Score $\boxed{}$

C Fractions and Decimals... Tick (✓) the correct answer.

1. $4·3 − 1·5 =$ a $2·8$ b $3·8$ c $5·8$ 6. $1·2 + 2·3 + 1·1 =$ a $4·6$ b $4·7$ c $5·6$

2. $0·2 + 0·9 + 1 =$ a $1·11$ b $1·1$ c $2·1$ 7. $3·4 − 1·2 − 0·1 =$ a $1·1$ b $2·1$ c $3·1$

3. $0·5$ of $15 =$ a $7·5$ b 30 c 75 8. $3·6 − 2 + 0·4 =$ a 2 b 3 c 4

4. $\frac{1}{10}$ of $15 =$ a $1·5$ b 15 c 150 9. $1·6 + 1·8 − 2·3 =$ a $1·1$ b $2·9$ c $3·5$

5. $\frac{2}{3}$ of $6 =$ a 2 b 4 c 9 10. $\frac{1}{4}$ of $2 =$ a $0·2$ b $0·5$ c 1

Score $\boxed{}$

D Shapes, Measures and Data... Write the times that are 20 minutes later than the times shown.

1. 6:10 $\boxed{\ :\ }$ 5. 6:55 $\boxed{\ :\ }$ 9. 1:30 $\boxed{\ :\ }$

2. 2:25 $\boxed{\ :\ }$ 6. 1:10 $\boxed{\ :\ }$ 10. 7:35 $\boxed{\ :\ }$

3. 11:50 $\boxed{\ :\ }$ 7. 8:40 $\boxed{\ :\ }$

4. 9:45 $\boxed{\ :\ }$ 8. 5:05 $\boxed{\ :\ }$

Score $\boxed{}$

E Problem Solving

1. Dad spent €2·30, €1·60 and €0·90. How much in total did he spend?   € $\boxed{}$

2. Three children have a total age of 21. Two are 4 and 9. What age is the other? $\boxed{}$

3. A 3 m 90 cm string was cut into three equal pieces. What length is each piece? $\boxed{}$ m

4. How much will I save on a €12·80 ham if the price is reduced by $\frac{1}{4}$?   € $\boxed{}$

5. Bars are 40c each or 6 for €2. How much for 14 bars?   € $\boxed{}$

Give yourself 2 marks for each correct answer.   Score

Unit 23 - Quick Questions

A Tables

1. $7 + 8 =$ ☐
2. $9 + 6 =$ ☐
3. ☐ $- 9 = 10$
4. ☐ $- 5 = 7$
5. $10 +$ ☐ $= 20$
6. $8 \times 7 =$ ☐
7. $9 \times$ ☐ $= 81$
8. $4 \times$ ☐ $= 36$
9. $8 \div$ ☐ $= 4$
10. $63 \div 7 =$ ☐
11. $72 \div$ ☐ $= 8$
12. $48 \div$ ☐ $= 6$

B Calculate.

1. $103 + 55 + 24 =$ ☐
2. $83 - 32 + 19 =$ ☐
3. $26 + 33 + 14 =$ ☐
4. $264 + 654 - 22 =$ ☐
5. $147 + 312 + 13 =$ ☐
6. $272 - 43 =$ ☐
7. $12 \times 2 \times 4 =$ ☐
8. $625 \div 5 =$ ☐
9. €$3{\cdot}23 -$ €$1{\cdot}42 =$ € ☐
10. $0{\cdot}5 + 0{\cdot}5 + 0{\cdot}25 =$ ☐
11. $5 + 0{\cdot}5 + 0{\cdot}25 =$ ☐
12. $2{\cdot}5 + 0{\cdot}4 - 0{\cdot}5 =$ ☐

C Numbers... Are these numbers $>$ (greater than), $<$ (less than) or $=$ (equal to) each other?

1. $\frac{1}{4}$ of 12 ☐ $\frac{1}{3}$ of 12
2. $\frac{1}{3}$ of 18 ☐ $\frac{1}{2}$ of 12
3. $\frac{1}{4}$ of 12 ☐ $\frac{1}{2}$ of 18
4. $\frac{1}{3}$ of 18 ☐ $\frac{1}{4}$ of 12
5. $(9 \times 9) + 10$ ☐ 100
6. $(7 \times 8) - 6$ ☐ 50
7. $(11 \times 9) - 3$ ☐ 10×9
8. $3{\cdot}45 + 2{\cdot}13$ ☐ 5
9. 7×8 ☐ 12×6
10. $2 - 0{\cdot}5$ ☐ $1 + 0{\cdot}5$
11. $0{\cdot}2 + 0{\cdot}1 + 0{\cdot}1$ ☐ $0{\cdot}5$
12. €$2{\cdot}40 \div 2$ ☐ €$13{\cdot}00$

D Money... Find the cost of each shopping list.

Zoo ticket (Z) = 50c

TRAIN TICKET 30c
Train ticket (T) = 30c

Bus ticket (B) = 25c

1. $2Z + 1T + 1B =$ € ☐
2. $1Z + 1T + 2B =$ € ☐
3. $2Z + 1T + 3B =$ € ☐
4. $1Z + 1T + 4B =$ € ☐
5. $1Z + 1T + 1B =$ € ☐
6. $2Z + 3T + 1B =$ € ☐
7. $2Z + 2T + 1B =$ € ☐
8. $4Z + 3B =$ €€ ☐
9. $2Z + 3T =$ € ☐
10. $2Z + 1T + 2B =$ € ☐
11. $1Z + 4T + 1B =$ € ☐
12. $2Z + 2T + 2B =$ € ☐

E Figure it out. Use $+$, $-$, $\times$ or $\div$ to complete the number sentences.

1. 5 ☐ 5 ☐ $2 = 50$
2. $(5$ ☐ $1)$ ☐ $5 = 30$
3. $(12$ ☐ $3)$ ☐ $6 = 24$
4. $(6$ ☐ $7)$ ☐ $10 = 52$
5. $2{\cdot}25$ ☐ $1{\cdot}12 = 3{\cdot}37$
6. $(223$ ☐ $2)$ ☐ $10 = 436$
7. $(13$ ☐ $4)$ ☐ $2 = 18$
8. $5{\cdot}5$ ☐ 1 ☐ $2{\cdot}5 = 4$
9. $2{\cdot}5$ ☐ 2 ☐ $1 = 3{\cdot}5$
10. $4{\cdot}5$ ☐ 2 ☐ $1 = 3{\cdot}5$
11. $(9$ ☐ $3)$ ☐ $7 = 10$
12. $(11$ ☐ $3)$ ☐ $1 = 34$

Be careful! Some division sums have remainders.

A Work it out.

1.
```
    4 1
  x 2 3
```

2.
```
    4 4
  x 1 4
```

3.
```
    3 2
  x 1 8
```

4.
```
    5 6
  x 2 6
```

5.
```
    9 4
  x 1 5
```

6.
```
    2 6 6
    1 9 1
  + 4 0 0
```

7.
```
    2 9 2
    3 0 7
  + 1 3 8
```

8.
```
  1 7 7 3
  1 4 7 6
  +  3 8 8
```

9.
```
  1 6 6 7
    4 0 9
  +  8 3 4
```

10.
```
    5 2 3
  1 2 0 6
  +  9 7 4
```

11.
```
    2     3
      4 0
  +     2
    5 6 6
```

12.
```
    2     9
    1 4
  +   3 9
    5 5 5
```

13.
```
    1     7
        3 3
  +   2 7
    6 7 8
```

14.
```
    2     4
      4 8
  + 1 6
    5 6 0
```

15.
```
        1 2
    3     4
  +     5
    4 7 7
```

16.
```
  €3 ·3 3
  x       3
```

17.
```
  €4 ·6 8
  x       8
```

18.
```
  €9 ·8 7
  x       6
```

19.
```
  €6 ·3 7
  x       4
```

20.
```
  €5 ·2 9
  x       5
```

B Work it out.

1. 3 | 2 5 8

2. 4 | 7 0 6   R

3. 5 | 4 9 9   R

4. 6 | 7 2 8   R

5. 8 | 9 0 7   R

6.
hrs	mins
1	5 5
+ 1	1 0

7.
hrs	mins
1	2 0
+ 2	1 5

8.
hrs	mins
1	3 5
+ 1	2 0

9.
hrs	mins
1	4 0
+ 1	4 0

10.
hrs	mins
1	0 5
+ 1	2 5

11.
```
    7 3
  x 4 1
```

12.
```
    4 7
  x 3 7
```

13.
```
    4 8
  x 3 7
```

14.
```
    6 7
  x 3 9
```

15.
```
    4 8
  x 2 6
```

16.
kg	g
1	1 0 0
2	2 3 0
+ 2	2 5 5

17.
kg	g
3	5 0 0
1	2 5 0
+ 2	0 4 5

18.
kg	g
2	2 0 0
2	2 1 0
+ 1	1 2 0

19.
kg	g
1	2 5 0
3	2 5 0
+ 1	2 5 0

20.
kg	g
1	1 0 0
1	2 5 0
+ 2	4 0 0

A Figure it out. The ice-cream man sells 4 types of ice-cream.

	cone 90c		choc-ice 70c		ice-pop 55c		Cornetto 60c

1. On Tuesday, he sold 3 choc-ices and 4 cones. How much money did he get? € [   ]

2. On Friday, he sold 4 ice-pops and 3 cones. How much money did he get? € [   ]

3. Today he got €7·00 for 8 ice-creams. 7 were cones. What was the other? [   ]

4. Mary bought 3 ice-pops. Pat bought 2 cones. Who paid more money? [   ]

5. Tom spent exactly €2·20 on 3 ice-creams. What did he buy?
   [   ] , [   ] , [   ]

6. Jane bought 2 ice-creams. She got 20c change from €2·00. What did she buy?
   [   ] , [   ]

7. How much more would 5 Cornettos cost than 3 cones? € [   ]

8. Tom buys the same ice-cream on 4 days and spends €2·20. What is the ice-cream?
   [   ]

B Think it out. Tick (✓) the correct answer.

1. 3 boxes weigh 22·4 kg. A weighs 7 kg. B weighs 4·3 kg. What weight is C?
   a 10·7 kg b 11·1 kg c 11·7 kg

2. $\frac{3}{4}$ of the 16 children in 4th class have blue eyes. How many is that? a 4 b 8 c 12

3. There are 9 oranges in a net. How many in 8 nets? a 63 b 72 c 81

4. By how much is 4·42 kg less than 7 kg?
   a 2·42 kg b 2·58 kg c 3·58 kg

5. How many millilitres in a $\frac{1}{4}$ litre?
   a 25 ml b 75 ml c 250 ml

6. Tom is 139 cm tall. Mary is 12 cm taller. How tall is Mary?
   a 141 cm b 1·51 m c 151 m

7. $(12 \div 4) + 13$ [   ] $= (5 \times 4) - 3$
   a − 1 b + 1 c + 3

8. A €6·90 toy was reduced by $\frac{1}{2}$. How much is it now? a €3·45 b €10·35 c €12·80

C Puzzle it out. Do the sums and use the answers to crack the code.

U	825	T	713	D	851	K	506	L	768	H	459	O	960	A	396	I	324	Y	648	E	399	G	546

1. 37 x 23 = [   ]
2. 40 x 24 = [   ]
3. 36 x 18 = [   ]
4. 96 x 10 = [   ]

5. 55 x 15 = [   ]
6. 48 x 16 = [   ]
7. 18 x 18 = [   ]
8. 23 x 22 = [   ]

9. 21 x 19 = [   ]
10. 31 x 23 = [   ]
11. 48 x 20 = [   ]
12. 24 x 32 = [   ]

13. 22 x 18 = [   ]
14. 25 x 33 = [   ]
15. 39 x 14 = [   ]
16. 27 x 17 = [   ]

If you need to, you can work out these sums in your copy.

Sum No.	1	2	3	4	5	6	7	8	9	10	11	12	13	14	15	16
Answer																
Code																

★ **Score each exercise out of 10.**

A Tables

1. 3 + 8 = ☐
2. ☐ − 3 = 9
3. 17 − ☐ = 9
4. ☐ − 8 = 5
5. 6 x ☐ = 18
6. ☐ x 8 = 48
7. 9 x 6 = ☐
8. 56 ÷ 8 = ☐
9. ☐ ÷ 8 = 9
10. ☐ ÷ 8 = 8

Score ☐

B Computation

1.	hrs	mins	2.		8	2	3.		2	7	4.	€4	0	·3	9	5.			4	8
	1	2 5		− 4		0		x	3	8		− €1	7	·5	8		x		1	2
	1	3 0		1	9	2														
											+ €4	4	·0	6					
																	−	3 7 8	

Give yourself 2 marks for each correct sum. **Score** ☐

C Fractions and Decimals

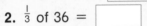

1. 0·5 of 44 = ☐
2. $\frac{1}{3}$ of 36 = ☐
3. $\frac{1}{5}$ of 3·5 = ☐
4. 0·9 + 0·3 + 0·6 = ☐
5. 2·3 − 1 + 0·6 = ☐
6. 1·2 + 1·4 + 1·4 = ☐
7. 1·8 − 1·2 + 2 = ☐
8. 4·3 − 1·8 + 0·7 = ☐
9. $\frac{1}{6}$ of 18 less $\frac{1}{5}$ of 10 = ☐
10. $\frac{2}{3}$ of 9 plus $\frac{1}{3}$ of 6 = ☐

Score ☐

D Shapes, Measures and Data... Ring the number or amount that does not belong.

1. $\frac{3}{4}$, 0.75, $\frac{1}{3}$
2. 25 g, 25c, €0·25
3. 0.75 kg, $\frac{3}{4}$ kg, 7·25 g
4. 250 secs, 2 mins 30 secs, $2\frac{1}{2}$ mins
5. 100 m, 0·1 kg, $\frac{1}{10}$ km

Give yourself 2 marks for each correct answer. **Score** ☐

E Problem Solving... Tick (✓) the correct answer.

1. How many 8s in 55? | a 6 | b 7 | c 8 |
2. How many grams in 2·5 kg? | a 25 g | b 250 g | c 2500 g |
3. By how much is 206 more than 140? | a 54 | b 64 | c 66 |
4. What is missing? 65 − 25 ▉ 6 x 7 | a > | b < | c = |
5. How much for 6 pens at 35c each? | a €1·55 | b €1·85 | c €2·10 |

Give yourself 2 marks for each correct answer. **Score** ☐

Unit 24 - Quick Questions

A Tables

1. 7 x ☐ = 56
2. ☐ x 5 = 50
3. 3 x ☐ = 27
4. ☐ x 8 = 56
5. 6 x ☐ = 42
6. 9 x ☐ = 81
7. 54 ÷ ☐ = 6
8. ☐ ÷ 3 = 4
9. 81 ÷ ☐ = 9
10. 49 ÷ ☐ = 7
11. ☐ ÷ 8 = 9
12. ☐ ÷ 9 = 9

B Calculate.

1. 47 + ☐ = 107
2. ☐ + 69 = 112
3. 76 + ☐ = 110
4. 312 − ☐ = 107
5. 128 − ☐ = 58
6. 68 − ☐ = 29
7. (4 x 7) + 12 = ☐
8. (8 x 3) + 14 = ☐
9. 696 ÷ 6 = ☐
10. 432 ÷ 8 = ☐
11. €3·69 + €2·21 = € ☐
12. €9·50 − €2·35 = € ☐

C Numbers... Order from largest to smallest.

1. 413, 341, 344 ☐ , ☐ , ☐
2. 79·2, 97·1, 89·8 ☐ , ☐ , ☐
3. $\frac{3}{4}$, $\frac{1}{2}$, $\frac{1}{4}$ ☐ , ☐ , ☐
4. $\frac{2}{10}$, $\frac{2}{5}$, $\frac{2}{3}$ ☐ , ☐ , ☐
5. 52·7, 51·9, 51·5 ☐ , ☐ , ☐
6. 63·6, 64·1, 64·6 ☐ , ☐ , ☐
7. 226, 261, 216 ☐ , ☐ , ☐
8. 41 + 5, 44 − 3, 43 + 4 ☐ , ☐ , ☐
9. 25 − 2, 21 + 1, 23 − 3 ☐ , ☐ , ☐
10. 16·3, 16·6, 16·7 ☐ , ☐ , ☐
11. 3·6, 3·8, 4·2 ☐ , ☐ , ☐
12. 40 − 5, 35 + 6, 38 + 2 ☐ , ☐ , ☐

D Money... Write the totals as euros and cents.

1. 137c + 50c − 10c = € ☐
2. 208c + 60c − 25c = € ☐
3. 307c + 99c − 15c = € ☐
4. 48c + 160c − 20c = € ☐
5. 77c + 99c + 99c = € ☐
6. 460c + 70c + 21c = € ☐
7. 299c + 112c − 50c = € ☐
8. 410c + 50c − 23c = € ☐
9. 198c + 98c + 98c = € ☐
10. 128c − 60c + 55c = € ☐
11. 63c + 45c + 11c = € ☐
12. 88c + 20c + 19c = € ☐

E Figure it out. True (✔) or false (✗)?

1. 39 is divisible by 3. ☐
2. 84 is a multiple of 8. ☐
3. $\frac{1}{6}$ of 54 is 7. ☐
4. $\frac{1}{5}$ of 45 is 9. ☐
5. 23 is one-third of 69. ☐
6. It is dark at 11:45 a.m. ☐
7. A sphere is the same as two circles. ☐
8. $\frac{2}{3}$ is greater than $\frac{1}{4}$. ☐
9. 1·75 + 1·5 = 2·25 ☐
10. 5·7 > 7·5 ☐
11. $\frac{1}{10}$ of 90 is 45. ☐
12. €4·50 ÷ 3 = €2·50 ☐

A Work it out.

1.	5 6 x 8	2.	6 3 x 7	3.	8 9 x 6	4.	9 5 x 4	5.	6 7 x 9

6.
```
  7 2 2
  4 6 2
+   8 2
```

7.
```
  5 2 4
    5 5
+ 1 9 4
```

8.
```
    8 8
    7 2
+ 6 5 5
```

9.
```
  4 8 9
  2 5 7
+   8 6
```

10.
```
  3 0 9
  1 8 8
+ 3 5 1
```

11.
```
  4 5 6
  2 1
+     2
  8 0 7
```

12.
```
    5 3
  6 1
+ 1   6
  9 1 7
```

13.
```
  2   9
    4 0
+ 1   4
  5 9 3
```

14.
```
    5 6
  3 7
+     4
  6 2 8
```

15.
```
    0 7
  2   3
+   6
  5 9 4
```

16. 4)€1·24 17. 6)€2·34 18. 8)€4·88 19. 9)€3·42 20. 7)€7·21

B Work it out.

1. 5)6 0 7 2. 8)3 7 9 3. 6)4 0 2 4. 9)9 9 2 5. 6)2 0 8

    R   R   R   R

6.
```
  €4 5 ·3 3
+ €3 2 ·6 6

- €1 0 ·0 1
```

7.
```
  €2 2 ·7 1
+ €6 3 ·4 4

-   €9 ·4 5
```

8.
```
  €7 1 ·4 7
+   €9 ·5 9

- €4 4 ·6 5
```

9.
```
  €2 7 ·2 7
+ €3 8 ·4 8

- €4 5 ·6 6
```

10.
```
  €4 8 ·3 9
+ €1 7 ·0 5

- €2 7 ·8 8
```

11.
```
  m  cm
  1  3 5
  2  1 4
+ 2  0 6
```

12.
```
  m  cm
  1  4 0
  1  2 7
+ 2  0 6
```

13.
```
  m  cm
  2  2 5
  1  4 9
+ 1  4 0
```

14.
```
  m  cm
  2  1 0
  1  2 5
+ 2  3 5
```

15.
```
  m  cm
  2  3 5
  1  5 0
+ 1  2 9
```

16.
```
    4 6
  x 5 3
```

17.
```
    7 8
  x 2 7
```

18.
```
    4 8
  x 5 3
```

19.
```
    2 8
  x 6 4
```

20.
```
    8 2
  x 5 6
```

April 2015

Mon	Tue	Wed	Thur	Fri	Sat	Sun
		1	2	3	4	5
6	7	8	9	10	11	12
13	14	15	16	17	18	19
20	21	22	23	24	25	26
27	28	29	30			

May 2015

Mon	Tue	Wed	Thur	Fri	Sat	Sun
				1	2	3
4	5	6	7	8	9	10
11	12	13	14	15	16	17
18	19	20	21	22	23	24
25	26	27	28	29	30	31

June 2015

Mon	Tue	Wed	Thur	Fri	Sat	Sun
1	2	3	4	5	6	7
8	9	10	11	12	13	14
15	16	17	18	19	20	21
22	23	24	25	26	27	28
29	30					

A Use the calendar to answer the questions.

1. How many days:

   (a) in April? ☐

   (b) in May? ☐

   (c) in June? ☐

   (d) in May and June? ☐

2. On what day of the week is:

   (a) April 24th? ☐

   (b) May 24th? ☐

   (c) June 24th? ☐

   (d) March 31st? ☐

3. Which month:

   (a) has 5 Mondays? ☐

   (b) has 5 Sundays? ☐

   (c) has 5 Tuesdays? ☐

   (d) begins on Friday? ☐

B Use the calendar to find the correct dates.

1. 4th class school tour on the second Friday in April. Date: 10th

2. Cake sale on the last Tuesday in May. Date: ☐

3. Twins' birthday party on the third Sunday of June. Date: ☐

4. School holidays on the last Friday in June. Date: ☐

5. Sports Day on the second last Saturday in May. Date: ☐

6. Book sale on the second Wednesday in June. Date: ☐

7. School drama on the last Saturday in April. Date: ☐

8. Party for Grandad on the second Saturday in June. Date: ☐

C Fruity O'Rooney loves fruit. How much did he pay for fruit in April, May and June?

€1·15 per kg	€1·25 per kg	20 c 6 for €1	15c 8 for €1	25c 5 for €1	10c 12 for €1	35c 3 for €1	€1·30 2 for €2·50

April	
3 kg grapes	€
2 pineapples	€
6 oranges	€
12 apples	€
Total	€

May	
14 apples	€
3 kg grapes	€
18 pears	€
25 kiwis	€
Total	€

June	
4 kg bananas	€
10 oranges	€
13 kiwis	€
7 grapefruits	€
Total	€

Unit 24 - Check-up

A Tables

1. 12 x 7 = ☐
2. ☐ x 11 = 44
3. 8 x 12 = ☐
4. 16 − 5 = ☐
5. 14 − ☐ = 11
6. ☐ − 12 = 7
7. ☐ ÷ 4 = 12
8. ☐ ÷ 11 = 8
9. ☐ ÷ 5 = 9
10. 60 ÷ 5 = ☐

Score ☐

B Computation

1.		1	9	9
		5	0	8
	+	3	1	7

2.	6	4	0	2
	x			4

3.		m	cm
		2	58
		3	18
	+		39

4.	€2	0	·5	0
	− €1	6	·9	9
	x			7

5.		4	1	7
	+	3	6	6
	3			

Give yourself 2 marks for each correct sum. **Score** ☐

C Fractions and Decimals... Choose a correct answer from the list for each question.

0·3   2·5   0·7   3·5   1·5   0·5   0·4   0·1   0·6   2

1. 1·5 + 2 = ☐
2. $\frac{7}{10}$ = ☐
3. $\frac{1}{10}$ = ☐
4. 3 − 1·5 = ☐
5. 1 − 0·4 = ☐
6. 0·7 − 0·2 = ☐
7. $\frac{3}{10}$ = ☐
8. 1 − 0·6 = ☐
9. 1·2 + 1·3 = ☐
10. 3 − 1·5 + 0·5 = ☐

Score ☐

D Shapes, Measures and Data... Write **time**, **capacity**, **weight**, **speed**, or **distance**.

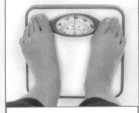

1. _____
2. _____
3. _____
4. _____
5. _____

Give yourself 2 marks for each correct answer. **Score** ☐

E Problem Solving

It was a hot day. 16 people bought ice-creams. One-quarter of them bought cones. Half the cones had a flake in them. The cones cost 80c and the flakes were 20c extra. Half bought ice-pops. The ice-pops were 40c. The others bought a nutty ice-cream.

1. How many people bought a cone? ☐
2. How many people bought ice-pops? ☐
3. How many people bought a nutty ice-cream? ☐
4. How much was paid in total for cones and flakes? € ☐
5. How much was paid in total for ice-pops? € ☐

Give yourself 2 marks for each correct answer. **Score** ☐

Unit 25 - Quick Questions

A Tables

1. $10 + \boxed{} = 17$
2. $8 + 9 = \boxed{}$
3. $14 - \boxed{} = 6$
4. $16 - 7 = \boxed{}$
5. $8 + 9 = \boxed{}$
6. $8 \times 7 = \boxed{}$
7. $9 \times 9 = \boxed{}$
8. $10 \times 6 = \boxed{}$
9. $36 \div 4 = \boxed{}$
10. $54 \div 6 = \boxed{}$
11. $63 \div 7 = \boxed{}$
12. $32 \div 8 = \boxed{}$

B Calculate.

1. $28 + \boxed{} + 25 = 78$
2. $34 + \boxed{} + 37 = 80$
3. $20 + \boxed{} + 22 = 67$
4. $35 + \boxed{} + 25 = 88$
5. $80 - \boxed{} = 31$
6. $60 - \boxed{} = 29$
7. $(7 \times 8) - 5 = \boxed{}$
8. $(9 \times 5) + 8 = \boxed{}$
9. $384 \div 6 = \boxed{}$
10. $(27 \div 9) - 2 = \boxed{}$
11. $(72 \div 9) + 8 = \boxed{}$
12. $\boxed{} - 2 \cdot 4 = 1 \cdot 5$

C Numbers... Complete the tables.

Tables	1	2	3	4	5	6	7	8	9	10
x 3										
x 6										
x 7										
x 9										

D Fractions

1. $\frac{1}{2}$ of 12 plus $\frac{1}{3}$ of 6 = $\boxed{}$
2. $\frac{1}{3}$ of 9 plus $\frac{1}{3}$ of 6 = $\boxed{}$
3. $\frac{1}{4}$ of 20 plus $\frac{1}{2}$ of 24 = $\boxed{}$
4. $\frac{1}{4}$ of 12 plus $\frac{1}{6}$ of 12 = $\boxed{}$
5. $\frac{2}{3}$ of 9 plus $\frac{1}{4}$ of 4 = $\boxed{}$
6. $\frac{1}{2}$ of 18 plus $\frac{3}{4}$ of 8 = $\boxed{}$

7. $\frac{1}{2}$ of 30 plus $\frac{1}{4}$ of 8 = $\boxed{}$
8. $\frac{1}{4}$ of 16 plus $\frac{1}{3}$ of 18 = $\boxed{}$
9. $\frac{1}{4}$ of 20 less $\frac{1}{3}$ of 9 = $\boxed{}$
10. $\frac{1}{3}$ of 18 less $\frac{1}{4}$ of 16 = $\boxed{}$
11. $\frac{3}{4}$ of 44 = $\boxed{}$
12. $\frac{2}{3}$ of 33 = $\boxed{}$

E Figure it out. Tick (✓) the correct answer.

1. $(6 \times 7) + 10 =$ a 42   b 48   c 52
2. $(72 \div 8) - 2 =$ a 9   b 7   c 5
3. $(2 \times 3 \times 4) + 1 =$ a 7   b 13   c 25
4. $(42 \div 6) + 3 =$ a 7   b 10   c 13
5. €5·65 − €2·30 =   a €2·35   b €2·95   c €3·35
6. €1·27 + €2·42 =   a €3·29   b €2·62   c €3·69
7. $\frac{1}{3}$ of 30 + $\frac{1}{4}$ of 20 =   a 10   b 15   c 20
8. $\frac{1}{5}$ of 10 + $\frac{1}{4}$ of 32 =   a 10   b 12   c 15
9. $\frac{1}{5}$ of €4·50 =   a €9·00   b €4·70   c €0·90
10. $\frac{1}{5}$ of €5·20 =   a €1·04   b €1·20   c €1·40

11. $2 \cdot 3 + 4 \cdot 5 + 1 \cdot 7 =$ a 7·35   b 7·5   c 8·5
12. $6 \cdot 2 + 1 \cdot 7 - 2 \cdot 5 =$ a 5·4   b 9·9   c 10·4

A Work it out.

1.		2		2.			2	3.		4	4.			1	5.		2
x		3		x			2	x		7	x			5	x		6
	7	8				8	4		2 8 0			4 0 5				1 3 2

6.			7	8	7.		3	7	8	8.		4	3	3	9.		4	2	2	10.		2	4	2
		1	0	8			1	2	7			3	4	5			2	8	8			1	3	8
+	3	9	8		+	2	6	6		+	3	7	2		+	3	6	0		+	7	0	0	

11.		7	0	8	12.		5	1	2	13.		4	1	3	14.		7	1	2	15.		3	2	1
−	3	4	7		−	3	4	6		−		9	9		−	3	5	4		−	2	0	7	

16.			2	5	17.			1	6	18.			2	7	19.			3	3	20.			4	5
	x	2	5			x	1	6			x	2	7			x	3	3			x	4	5	

B Work it out.

1.	6	2 6 7	2.	7	2 3 7	3.	4	3 5 1	4.	9	2 4 2	5.	8	4 0 6
		R			R			R			R			R

6. kg		g	7. kg		g	8. kg		g	9. kg		g	10. kg		g
2	1	5 0	1	1	2 0		7	5 0	2	0	8 0	1	3	5 0
1	2	5 0	2	1	5 5	1	5	0 0	2	1	5 0	1	2	0 0
+ 1	1	2 5	+ 2	1	2 5	+ 1	2	7 5	+ 1	1	5 5	+ 1	1	7 5

11.		5	7	12.		3	6	13.		2	8	14.		3	4	15.		3	7
	x	2	6		x	2	3		x	4	3		x	4	2		x	4	3

16.	2	8	·6	17.	3	5	·4	18.	2	9	·2	19.	3	1	·4	20.	2	3	·5
−	1	7	·9	−	1	0	·8	−	1	0	·6	−	1	5	·6	−	1	7	·8

Unit 25 - Problems

A Figure it out.

1. A bag of flour weighs 2·2 kg. How much will $3\frac{1}{2}$ bags weigh? ☐ kg
2. Eggs cost €1·80 for 6. How much for 15 eggs? € ☐
3. 2 cats had 4 kittens each and 1 cat had 5 kittens. How many kittens in total? ☐
4. Pat spent €3·57 in the shop. How much change did he get from €10·50? € ☐
5. John is 1·8 m tall and he is 0·15 m taller than Tom. What height is Tom? ☐ m
6. Liam gets up at 7:45 a.m, 20 mins before Dónal. What time does Dónal get up? ☐ : ☐ a.m.
7. A pack of rashers weighs 0·5 kg. How much do 7 packs weigh? ☐ kg
8. Jake had €3·90 and bought 4 ice-creams at 95c each. How much had he left? € ☐
9. A boy and two girls have a total age of 20. The girls are 3 and 8. What age is the boy? ☐
10. A triangle has three equal-length sides. What is the perimeter if one side is 6 cm? ☐ cm

B Think it out. Tick (✓) the correct answer.

1. Ted has 3 fewer sweets than Mary. Ted has 9. Mary has [a] 3 [b] 6 [c] 12
2. A school has 67 girls and 36 boys. How many in total is that? [a] 113 [b] 103 [c] 93
3. A train left at 2:30 p.m. It arrived at 3:15 p.m. The journey took [a] 45 mins [b] 65 mins [c] 85 mins
4. Apples are 6c each or 6 for 30c. How much for 13 apples? [a] 36c [b] 66c [c] 78c
5. 65 – 14 ☐ 5 x 10 [a] > [b] < [c] =
6. How many legs in total have 4 dogs and 5 ducks? [a] 16 [b] 26 [c] 36
7. How many people on a train with 4 carriages and 9 people in each? [a] 13 [b] 27 [c] 36
8. By how much is 366 greater than 143? [a] 123 [b] 134 [c] 223
9. 3 boxes had 26, 33 and 43 oranges. How many altogether? [a] 92 [b] 102 [c] 109
10. The total age of triplets is 18. The age of one of them is [a] 3 [b] 6 [c] 9

C Puzzle it out. Use the 100-square to complete the tasks.

1. Ring every 9th number, starting with 9.
2. Write 5 multiples of 10. ☐, ☐, ☐, ☐, ☐
3. What number is 24 greater than 59? ☐
4. Put a line through every 8th number, starting at 8 and ending at 48.
5. Write 5 multiples of 6. ☐, ☐, ☐, ☐, ☐
6. Start at 73 and count back 14 to ☐.
7. Put an x on any number that is a multiple of 7.
8. Count backwards in 6s, starting at 60.
   ☐, ☐, ☐, ☐, ☐, ☐, ☐, ☐
9. Write four numbers that divide evenly into 36. ☐, ☐, ☐, ☐
10. Write four numbers that divide evenly into 30. ☐, ☐, ☐, ☐

1	2	3	4	5	6	7	8	9	10
11	12	13	14	15	16	17	18	19	20
21	22	23	24	25	26	27	28	29	30
31	32	33	34	35	36	37	38	39	40
41	42	43	44	45	46	47	48	49	50
51	52	53	54	55	56	57	58	59	60
61	62	63	64	65	66	67	68	69	70
71	72	73	74	75	76	77	78	79	80
81	82	83	84	85	86	87	88	89	90
91	92	93	94	95	96	97	98	99	100

A Tables

1. $4 \times 8 = \boxed{}$
2. $72 \div 9 = \boxed{}$
3. $6 + \boxed{} = 15$
4. $\boxed{} - 7 = 8$
5. $8 \times 7 = \boxed{}$
6. $\boxed{} \div 9 = 5$
7. $9 \times \boxed{} = 54$
8. $63 \div 7 = \boxed{}$
9. $9 \times 9 = \boxed{}$
10. $42 \div \boxed{} = 6$

Score $\boxed{}$

B Computation

1.		4	1	7	2.			5	8	3.				6	7	4.	€2	9	·3	5	5.			3	2	7
	−	3	7	8		x			7				3		8		€4	0	·0	7		+		2	7	8
											+		1		2		+ €1	1	·4	4						
													7	5	4							−		4	7	6

Give yourself 2 marks for each correct sum.

Score $\boxed{}$

C Fractions and Decimals... Tick (✓) the correct answer.

1. $4\cdot6 + 0\cdot5 =$ a $4\cdot1$ b $4\cdot11$ c $5\cdot1$
2. $2\cdot5 - 0\cdot9 =$ a $1\cdot4$ b $1\cdot6$ c $3\cdot4$
3. $\frac{1}{10}$ of $45 =$ a $4\cdot5$ b 35 c 55
4. $\frac{1}{3}$ of $60 =$ a 20 b 27 c 93
5. $\frac{1}{7}$ of $21 =$ a 3 b 7 c 14

6. $1\cdot2 - 1 + 2\cdot2 =$ a $1\cdot2$ b $2\cdot2$ c $2\cdot4$
7. $3\cdot5 - 1\cdot5 + 1 =$ a 3 b $3\frac{1}{2}$ c $4\frac{1}{4}$
8. $3\cdot6 - 1 - 2\cdot3 =$ a $0\cdot3$ b $1\cdot3$ c $1\cdot6$
9. $1\cdot2 + 0\cdot9 + 1 =$ a $1\cdot3$ b $3\cdot1$ c $2\cdot2$
10. $\frac{1}{5}$ of $2\cdot5 =$ a $0\cdot5$ b $1\cdot25$ c 5

Score $\boxed{}$

D Shapes, Measures and Data

Write as kilograms and grams.

1. 1256 g $= \boxed{}$ kg $\boxed{}$ g
2. 3078 g $= \boxed{}$ kg $\boxed{}$ g
3. 692 g $= \boxed{}$ kg $\boxed{}$ g

How much change will I have from €10·00 if I spend:

4. €4·65 and €2·43?   € $\boxed{}$
5. €5·08 and €3·50?   € $\boxed{}$

Give yourself 2 marks for each correct answer.

Score $\boxed{}$

E Problem Solving

1. A plane left at 10:05 a.m. and arrived at 11:15 a.m.
   How long was the trip? $\boxed{}$ hrs $\boxed{}$ mins

2. A boy and his twin sisters have a total age of 31. He is 13.
   What age is each of his sisters? $\boxed{}$

3. A 3 m 45 cm string was cut into three equal pieces. What length is each piece? $\boxed{}$ m

4. Mum bought a €28·40 top for half price. How much did she pay?   € $\boxed{}$

5. Tickets are 55c each or 4 for €2. How much for 5 tickets?   € $\boxed{}$

Give yourself 2 marks for each correct answer.

Score $\boxed{}$

A Tables

1. 4 x [ ] = 28
2. [ ] x 7 = 63
3. 6 x [ ] = 36
4. [ ] x 9 = 36
5. 10 x [ ] = 70
6. 6 x [ ] = 42
7. 49 ÷ [ ] = 7
8. [ ] ÷ 4 = 6
9. 35 ÷ [ ] = 7
10. 81 ÷ [ ] = 9
11. [ ] x 5 = 35
12. [ ] x 8 = 56

B Calculate.

1. 25 + 35 + 30 = [ ]
2. 133 + 40 + 22 = [ ]
3. 422 + 40 + 15 = [ ]
4. 231 + 35 + 10 = [ ]
5. 388 – 58 = [ ]
6. 61 x 4 = [ ]
7. (84 ÷ 12) + 3 = [ ]
8. 96 ÷ 3 = [ ]
9. (11 x 4) + 12 = [ ]
10. (3 x 33) – 10 = [ ]
11. 7·5 + 2·3 = [ ]
12. 8·7 – [ ] = 3·4

C Numbers... Complete the sequences.

1. 57, 47, 37, [ ], [ ], [ ]
2. 6, 13, 20, [ ], [ ], [ ]
3. 16, 21, 26, [ ], [ ], [ ]
4. 8, 16, 24, [ ], [ ], [ ]
5. 17, 23, 29, [ ], [ ], [ ]
6. 49, 46, 43, [ ], [ ], [ ]
7. 15, 18, 21, [ ], [ ], [ ]
8. 64, 56, 48, [ ], [ ], [ ]
9. 1·6, 2·6, 3·6, [ ], [ ], [ ]
10. 88, 86, 84, [ ], [ ], [ ]
11. 2·3, 3·4, 4·5, [ ], [ ], [ ]
12. 6·5, 7, 7·5, [ ], [ ], [ ]

D Money... How much change from €10?

1. Spent €7·65. € [ ] left.
2. Spent €2·33. € [ ] left.
3. Spent €9·07. € [ ] left.
4. Spent €4·80. € [ ] left.
5. Spent €8·52. € [ ] left.
6. Spent €3·45. € [ ] left.
7. Spent €5·33. € [ ] left.
8. Spent €1·85. € [ ] left.
9. Spent €0·60. € [ ] left.
10. Spent €6·36. € [ ] left.
11. Spent €8·99. € [ ] left.
12. Spent €10·00. € [ ] left.

E Figure it out. Use +, −, x or ÷ to complete the number sentences.

1. 5 [ ] 2 [ ] 3 = 4
2. 8 [ ] 2 [ ] 3 = 13
3. (9 [ ] 5) [ ] 3 = 12
4. (4 [ ] 5) [ ] 2 = 18
5. (€3·30 [ ] 3) [ ] €0·10 = €10·00
6. (€5·50 [ ] €4·40) [ ] 2 = €2·20
7. (2 [ ] 3) [ ] 4 = 2
8. (7 [ ] 3) [ ] 2 = 8
9. (3 [ ] 11) [ ] 1 = 32
10. (12 [ ] 2) [ ] 5 = 29
11. (4 [ ] 3) [ ] 5 = 7
12. 25 [ ] 5 = 5

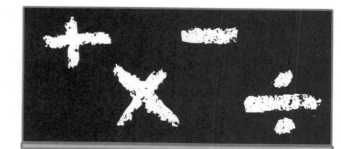

Be careful! Some division sums have remainders.

A Work it out.

```
1.      8 6       2.      7 4       3.      9 4       4.      6 9       5.      5 6
    x   5 4           x   7 5           x   3 6           x   3 9           x   4 9


6.    3 0 5       7.    5 0 2       8.    3 0 4       9.    2 0 9      10.  1 0 6 7
      1 4 4             1 4 5             1 7 7             1 4 3           1 4 3 2
    + 6 1 2           + 1 4 6           + 2 2 0           + 2 6 7         + 1 0 5 6


11.  2 6 5 1      12.  1 5 4 6      13.  3 2 7 0      14.    4 5 8      15.    7 3 8
   -   7 7 9         -   9 9 9         -   8 5 8         -   3 6 9         -   4 7 9


16.  8 | 4 8 7    17.  6 | 9 2 6    18.  9 | 9 0 3    19.  7 | 8 2 9    20.  8 | 6 2 8

              R                R                R                R                R
```

B Work it out.

```
1.      4   8    2.        8 2    3.      3 0      4.      4 1      5.      3 7
     -  2   0       -     7   0      -   1      2     -       4 9      -   1      7
        2 9 3             2 2 2          1 3 4            2 6 3            2 6 9


6.     €5 ·2 7   7.     €7 ·5 9   8.     €4 ·9 8   9.     €1 ·0 6  10.     €4 ·4 7
   x           3     x           6     x           5     x           4     x           7


11.    €8 ·1 4  12.     €9 ·2 7  13.     €4 ·3 3  14.     €1 ·9 3  15.     €6 ·3 7
   x           7     x           8     x           3     x           4     x           9


16.    4         17.    6         18.    2         19.    3         20.    4
           8               4             3 8             2 3                     6
     + 2 3           + 1 9           +     3           +     7           + 2 3
       8 6           1 0 7             8 9             9 9             1 0 2


21. €3 7 ·4 1   22. €3 8 ·1 9   23. €7 6 ·9 9   24. €7 8 ·8 8   25. €9 4 ·7 5
  - €1 7 ·8 2      -   €9 ·2 7     - €2 8 ·8 8     - €7 6 ·9 1     - €6 6 ·2 7
```

Unit 26 - Problems

A Figure it out.

> **A farmer has 8 cows, 12 sheep, 2 horses, 6 calves and a dog.**

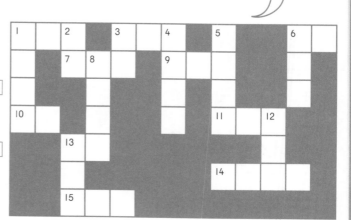

1. How many animals does the farmer have altogether? ☐
2. Each cow has 4 hooves. How many hooves altogether? ☐
3. How many eyes do the cows and the calves have altogether? ☐
4. The farmer keeps $\frac{1}{3}$ of the sheep in a shed. How many sheep are outside? ☐
5. If $\frac{1}{4}$ of the sheep and $\frac{1}{2}$ of the calves are sold, how many animals will be sold? ☐
6. The dog gets a 25c biscuit every day. What is the weekly cost? € ☐
7. How many more sheep than horses does the farmer have? ☐
8. The horses and $\frac{1}{2}$ of the cows drink in the river. How many animals is that? ☐
9. The farmer had €6·00. She spent €1·50, €1·10 and €0·40. How much is left? € ☐
10. $\frac{1}{2}$ of the farm animals (and the dog) love summer. How many love summer? ☐

B Think it out. Tick (✓) the correct answer.

1. What is the length of the side of a square if the perimeter is 28 cm?
   ☐ a 7 cm ☐ b 14 cm ☐ c 56 cm

2. 3 cakes cost €4·90. Two cost €2·10 and €1·40. How much was the 3rd?
   ☐ a €0·50 ☐ b €1·40 ☐ c €1·50

3. A pizza has ten slices. What fraction of the pizza is two slices? ☐ a $\frac{1}{5}$ ☐ b $\frac{2}{5}$ ☐ c $\frac{1}{10}$

4. What fraction is the same as 0·1?
   ☐ a $\frac{1}{2}$ ☐ b $\frac{1}{8}$ ☐ c $\frac{1}{10}$

5. 5 magazines cost €6·50. How much for 6 magazines? ☐ a €1·30 ☐ b €7·80 ☐ c €39·00

6. What total height in cm are two people who are 1·32 m and 1·49 m?
   ☐ a 28·1 m ☐ b 2·81 m ☐ c 281 m

7. By how much is 550 g less than 1 kg?
   ☐ a 450 g ☐ b 549 g ☐ c 1·55 kg

8. Joe bought a $\frac{1}{4}$ litre carton of milk. How many ml is that? ☐ a 250 ml ☐ b 750 ml ☐ c 250 l

9. What is missing? 47 − 16 + 9 = (6 x 7) ☐
   ☐ a + 4 ☐ b − 4 ☐ c − 2

10. 36 children went to a match. $\frac{1}{6}$ did not play. How many played? ☐ a 6 ☐ b 24 ☐ c 30

C Puzzle it out. Do the sums and complete the cross-number puzzle.

> If you need to, you can work out these sums in your copy.

Across
1. 456 − 348 = ☐
3. 209 x 4 = ☐
6. 8 x 5 = ☐
7. 24 x 6 = ☐
9. 213 x 3 = ☐
10. 9 x 7 = ☐
11. 839 − 426 = ☐
13. 11 x 8 = ☐
14. 2099 + 2064 = ☐
15. 122 x 4 = ☐

Down
1. 1067 + 859 = ☐
2. 9 x 9 = ☐
3. 12 x 7 = ☐
4. 3468 + 3177 = ☐
5. 5668 − 2734 = ☐
6. 81 x 6 = ☐
8. 1456 + 2872 = ☐
12. 768 − 442 = ☐
13. 211 x 4 = ☐

Unit 26 - Check-up

A Tables

1. $6 + 9 =$ ⬚

2. ⬚ $- 8 = 7$

3. $18 -$ ⬚ $= 8$

4. ⬚ $- 6 = 11$

5. $8 \times$ ⬚ $= 64$

6. ⬚ $\times 6 = 54$

7. $9 \times 8 =$ ⬚

8. $48 \div 8 =$ ⬚

9. $27 \div 3 =$ ⬚

10. ⬚ $\div 6 = 5$

Score ⬚

B Computation

1.		2	8	6
		3	4	7
	+	1	9	0

2.				0
	−	2		7
		2	4	6

3.			4	6
		×	2	5

4.	€3	9	·0	4
	− €2	0	·6	7
	+ €2	6	·4	4

5.			5	6
		×	6	4
		+ 4	1	2

Give yourself 2 marks for each correct sum.   Score ⬚

C Fractions and Decimals

1. $\frac{3}{10}$ of $100 =$ ⬚

2. $\frac{2}{3}$ of $24 =$ ⬚

3. $\frac{1}{3}$ of $9 =$ ⬚

4. $0·9 - 0·5 =$ ⬚

5. $2·5 - 2 + 0·3 =$ ⬚

6. $2·6 - 1·3 + 3 =$ ⬚

7. $1·2 + 2·7 - 0·5 =$ ⬚

8. $3·3 - 1·2 - 0·3 =$ ⬚

9. $\frac{1}{8}$ of 16 plus $\frac{1}{6}$ of $12 =$ ⬚

10. $\frac{1}{10}$ of 20 plus $\frac{1}{3}$ of $9 =$ ⬚

Score ⬚

D Shapes, Measures and Data... Name the shapes.

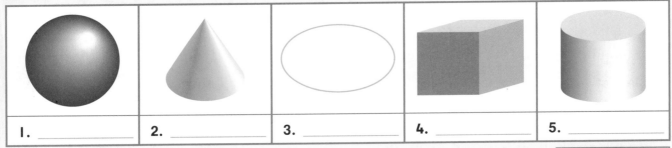

1. _____

2. _____

3. _____

4. _____

5. _____

Give yourself 2 marks for each correct answer.   Score ⬚

E Problem Solving... Tick (✓) the correct answer.

1. How many 7s in 64?   a ☐ 7   b ☐ 8   c ☐ 9

2. How many angles in a rectangle?   a ☐ 3   b ☐ 4   c ☐ 6

3. By how much is 107 less than 190?   a ☐ 47   b ☐ 83   c ☐ 65

4. What is missing? $57 - 12$ ▨ $11 \times 5 =$ a ☐ >   b ☐ =   c ☐ <

5. How much for 9 pencils at 25c each?   a ☐ €2·25   b ☐ €1·80   c ☐ €1·60

Give yourself 2 marks for each correct answer.   Score ⬚

Unit 27 - Quick Questions

A. Tables

1. $9 + 5 = \boxed{}$
2. $9 + 8 = \boxed{}$
3. $17 - 9 = \boxed{}$
4. $16 - \boxed{} = 7$
5. $8 + 5 = \boxed{}$
6. $9 \times 7 = \boxed{}$
7. $9 \times 5 = \boxed{}$
8. $6 \times 9 = \boxed{}$
9. $72 \div \boxed{} = 8$
10. $48 \div 6 = \boxed{}$
11. $63 \div \boxed{} = 7$
12. $54 \div \boxed{} = 6$

B. Calculate.

1. $37 + \boxed{} = 86$
2. $52 + \boxed{} = 91$
3. $46 + \boxed{} = 84$
4. $55 + \boxed{} = 72$
5. $96 - \boxed{} = 48$
6. $87 - \boxed{} = 54$
7. $(4 \times 7) + 2 = \boxed{}$
8. $(8 \times 8) + 4 = \boxed{}$
9. $(4 \times 20) + 8 = \boxed{}$
10. $(3 \times 20) - 5 = \boxed{}$
11. €4·37 $- \boxed{} =$ €1·99
12. €8·50 $- \boxed{} =$ €3·01

C. Numbers… Are these numbers > (greater than), < (less than) or = (equal to) each other?

1. $\frac{1}{6}$ of 12 $\boxed{}$ $\frac{1}{3}$ of 12
2. $\frac{1}{6}$ of 18 $\boxed{}$ $\frac{1}{3}$ of 3
3. $\frac{2}{3}$ of 9 $\boxed{}$ $\frac{1}{2}$ of 8
4. $\frac{1}{4}$ of 16 $\boxed{}$ $\frac{1}{5}$ of 10
5. $(4 \times 5) + 8$ $\boxed{}$ 5×6
6. $(3 \times 7) + 7$ $\boxed{}$ 4×7
7. $(12 \div 3) - 1$ $\boxed{}$ 2×4
8. $4·6 - 2·2$ $\boxed{}$ $2·5$
9. 9×5 $\boxed{}$ 6×7
10. $1 - 0·5$ $\boxed{}$ $0·6 - 0·3$
11. $0·3 + 0·3 + 0·3$ $\boxed{}$ 1
12. €36·40 $\div 4$ $\boxed{}$ €10·00 $-$ €0·50

D. Fractions

1. half of 124 = $\boxed{}$
2. one-fifth of 100 = $\boxed{}$
3. one-quarter of 48 = $\boxed{}$
4. one-third of 60 = $\boxed{}$
5. half of 64 = $\boxed{}$
6. one-quarter of 64 = $\boxed{}$

7. one-tenth of 90 = $\boxed{}$
8. one-third of 90 = $\boxed{}$
9. two-thirds of 90 = $\boxed{}$
10. one-tenth of 50 = $\boxed{}$
11. three-tenths of 100 = $\boxed{}$
12. four-tenths of 20 = $\boxed{}$

E. Figure it out. True (✓) or false (✗)?

1. 29 is divisible by 7. $\boxed{}$
2. 54 is a multiple of 9. $\boxed{}$
3. $\frac{1}{2}$ of €28·50 is €14·25. $\boxed{}$
4. $\frac{1}{8}$ of 40 is 4. $\boxed{}$
5. 10 is one-third of 36. $\boxed{}$
6. 11:50 p.m. is almost midnight. $\boxed{}$
7. 3, 4 and 6 are fractions. $\boxed{}$
8. 0·45 is greater than 0·4. $\boxed{}$

9. $3·25 + 0·75 = 3$ $\boxed{}$
10. $24 < \frac{1}{2}$ of 50 $\boxed{}$
11. $\frac{1}{4}$ of 10 is 2. $\boxed{}$
12. 53c = €0·53 $\boxed{}$

Be careful! Some division sums have remainders.

Unit 27 - Simply Sums

A Work it out.

1.		€5	·3	5	2.		€2	·6	6	3.		€6	·2	7	4.		€6	·4	5	5.		€9	·2	3
	x			3		x			5		x			6		x			4		x			6

6.	€9	2	·2	6	7.	€1	2	·2	8	8.	€4	3	·4	2	9.	€5	4	·2	6	10.	€6	4	·6	0
− €6	9	·5	6	−	€4	·0	8	− €1	5	·2	6	− €1	6	·3	8	− €2	8	·2	3					

11.	3	0	0	6	12.	3	0	8	6	13.		5	0	3	14.		4	1	2	15.		7	0	3
− 1	6	8	2	− 2	6	4	7	−	2	7	4	−	2	8	8	−	5	6	4					

16. 6 | 8 2 5   17. 9 | 4 6 6   18. 5 | 4 9 2   19. 6 | 3 1 8   20. 7 | 2 5 7

R (16), R (17), R (18), R (20)

B Work it out.

1.	2 9 2 0	2.	3 1 3 4	3.	3 1 5 6	4.	3 9 1 3	5.	1 0 9 2
	1 5 6 7		1 8 8 8		3 2 4 2		2 0 6 6		2 4 8 9
+	2 4 2 3	+	1 4 0 7	+	1 0 4 4	+	1 8 4 2	+	1 6 7 5

6.	2 1 8	7.	3 5 5	8.	7 2 2	9.	3 8 8	10.	4 0 8
+	3 7 8	+	4 0 3	+	1 9 9	+	2 6 9	+	4 8 2
−	3 0 3	−	2 6 6	−	1 5 6	−	4 0 3	−	5 1 4

11.	3 4 4	12.	2 5 7	13.	6 0 2	14.	4 0 3	15.	1 2 5
x	6	x	3	x	5	x	4	x	3

16.	2 9	17.	4 7	18.	3 8	19.	2 6	20.	4 4
x	1 4	x	3 4	x	2 9	x	1 8	x	2 6

21. 6 | 7 1 6   22. 9 | 3 9 9   23. 5 | 8 0 6   24. 6 | 4 7 7   25. 8 | 2 6 6

R (21), R (22), R (23), R (24), R (25)

A Making Shapes: Summer Shapes... Draw and colour these summer images using only regular shapes.

1. A sailing boat

2. Ice-creams

3. Two seagulls

4. An underwater scene

5. Shapes in the sky on a sunny day

6. Three interesting seaside toys

Unit 27 - Check-up

A Tables

1. $5 \times 9 =$ ☐
2. ☐ $\times 8 = 56$
3. $7 \times 9 =$ ☐
4. $19 - 10 =$ ☐
5. $17 -$ ☐ $= 11$
6. ☐ $- 9 = 5$
7. ☐ $\div 6 = 12$
8. ☐ $\div 8 = 6$
9. ☐ $\div 5 = 6$
10. $60 \div 6 =$ ☐

Score ☐

B Computation

1.		1	5	8
		4	0	9
	+	4	7	9

2.	6	6	9	0
	x			7

3.		m	cm
		4	2 0
		2	0 9
	+	3	0 0

4.	€2	3	·4	0
−	€1	9	·0	7
x				8

5.		5	9	0
	−	4	7	4
	2			

Give yourself 2 marks for each correct sum.

Score ☐

C Fractions and Decimals... Ring the correct amount.

1.	$\frac{7}{10}$	✦ ✦ ✦ ✦ ✦ ✦ ✦ ✦ ✦ ✦	6.	$\frac{3}{5}$	(bicycles ×15)
2.	0·7	(houses ×10)	7.	$\frac{2}{5}$	(smiley faces ×10)
3.	$\frac{1}{6}$	(ears ×18)	8.	0·25	(flags ×8)
4.	$\frac{2}{3}$	(trucks ×15)	9.	$\frac{1}{2}$	(hearts ×15)
5.	0·5	(cars ×13)	10.	$\frac{3}{4}$	(ribbons ×9)

Score ☐

D Shapes, Measures and Data

I had €7·00 but I only have €2·50 left.

How much did I spend?

1. €2·25 and € ☐
2. €3·40 and € ☐

Which measure is greater:

3. 2 kg 13 g or 2 kg 130 g? ☐ kg ☐ g
4. 1·5 l or 500 ml? ☐
5. 200 m or 1 km? ☐

Give yourself 2 marks for each correct answer.

Score ☐

E Problem Solving

90 people were at a hurling match. One-third of those people were playing on the two teams. The team players were aged 10, 11 or 12. Half of the players were 11 years old. One-tenth were 12 years old. The rest were 10 years old.

1. How many people were playing in the match? ☐
2. How many were on each team? ☐
3. How many players were 11 years old? ☐
4. How many were 12 years old? ☐
5. How many were 10 years old? ☐

Give yourself 2 marks for each correct answer.

Score ☐

Unit 28 - Quick Questions

A Tables

1. $4 \times \boxed{} = 24$
2. $\boxed{} \times 9 = 54$
3. $3 \times \boxed{} = 27$
4. $\boxed{} \times 7 = 49$
5. $10 \times \boxed{} = 100$
6. $8 \times \boxed{} = 24$
7. $64 \div \boxed{} = 8$
8. $\boxed{} \div 8 = 5$
9. $80 \div \boxed{} = 10$
10. $16 \div \boxed{} = 8$
11. $\boxed{} \div 6 = 7$
12. $\boxed{} \div 7 = 7$

B Calculate.

1. $(3 \times 3) + (2 \times 6) = \boxed{}$
2. $(6 \times 6) + (4 \times 6) = \boxed{}$
3. $(9 \times 3) - (4 \times 3) = \boxed{}$
4. $(3 \times 11) - (2 \times 10) = \boxed{}$
5. $678 - \boxed{} = 345$
6. $465 - \boxed{} = 265$
7. $(7 \times 6) + \boxed{} = 45$
8. $(5 \times 5) + \boxed{} = 27$
9. $(3 \times 7) + \boxed{} = 25$
10. $427 \div 7 = \boxed{}$
11. $568 \div 8 = \boxed{}$
12. $248 \div 4 = \boxed{}$

C Numbers... Complete the sequences.

1. 42, 45, 48, ___, ___, ___
2. 13, 18, 23, ___, ___, ___
3. 77, 72, 67, ___, ___, ___
4. 3, 9, 15, ___, ___, ___
5. 50, 46, 42, ___, ___, ___
6. 90, 81, 72, ___, ___, ___
7. 16, 22, 28, ___, ___, ___
8. 96, 84, 72, ___, ___, ___
9. 0·25, 0·5, 0·75, ___, ___, ___
10. 32, 40, 48, ___, ___, ___
11. 0·3, 0·6, 0·9, ___, ___, ___
12. 9, 8·5, 8, ___, ___, ___

D Money... How much change from €2?

 Stamp (S) = 50c

 Postcard (P) = 30c

1. 1S + 1P   Change = € 1·20
2. 2S + 1P   Change = € ___
3. 1S + 3P   Change = € ___
4. 4S   Change = € ___
5. 3S + 1P   Change = € ___
6. 1S + 4P   Change = € ___
7. 4P   Change = € ___
8. 1S + 2P   Change = € ___
9. 3S   Change = € ___
10. 5P   Change = € ___
11. 2S + 2P   Change = € ___
12. 3P   Change = € ___

E Figure it out. Tick (✓) the correct answer.

1. $(5 \times 5) - 11 =$ a 14 b 15 c 16
2. $(63 \div 7) + 2 =$ a 9 b 11 c 13
3. $(3 \times 3 \times 2) + 4 =$ a 18 b 22 c 24
4. $(35 \div 5) + 7 =$ a 7 b 10 c 14
5. $\frac{1}{6}$ of 12 + $\frac{1}{3}$ of 30 = a 12 b 14 c 16
6. $\frac{1}{5}$ of 15 + $\frac{1}{2}$ of 24 = a 13 b 15 c 17
7. $\frac{1}{5}$ of €11·50 = a €2·25 b €2·30 c €2·35
8. $\frac{1}{4}$ of €6·40 = a €0·80 b €1·60 c €3·20
9. $3·6 + 2·5 + 4·1 =$ a 5·4 b 9·9 c 10·2
10. $8·2 + 2·4 - 1·3 =$ a 8·9 b 9·3 c 10·6
11. €8·39 − €4·25 = a €4·14 b €4·64 c €12·64
12. €3·66 + €4·43 = a €1·23 b €7·23 c €8·09

Be careful! Some division sums have remainders.

Unit 28 – Simply Sums

A Work it out.

1.	2 4	2.	3 5	3.	2 0 6	4.	1 3 4	5.	4 2 4
x	5	x	6	x	7	x	4	x	8

6.	2 5 5	7.	3 2 2	8.	2 7 8	9.	2 9 9	10.	3 6 3
	3 7 8		1 6 5		3 4 8		3 0 8		1 9 8
+ 4 1 3		+ 5 0 4		+ 2 1 8		+ 1 4 9		+ 1 8 9	

11.	9 5 6	12.	5 2 0	13.	5 2 3	14.	4 8 4	15.	6 2 1
– 6 7 8		– 3 9 6		– 1 8 7		– 2 6 6		– 3 9 9	

16. 6)4 5 9   17. 7)4 5 9   18. 9)4 5 9   19. 8)4 5 9   20. 4)4 5 9

16. R   17. R   19. R   20. R

B Work it out.

1.	2 _ 3	2.	_ 2 7	3.	4 0 _	4.	4 3 _	5.	_ 1 7
– _ 1 6		– 5 8		– _ 2 6		– 2 _ 9		– 2 _ 9	
2 7 7		2 4 5		1 _ 4		_ 8 7		5 _ 1	

6.	€2 3 . 2 9	7.	€2 9 . 3 4	8.	€2 7 . 2 0	9.	€1 0 . 0 3	10.	€2 9 . 6 0
€3 4 . 4 3		€1 9 . 7 4		€3 7 . 4 5		€2 8 . 5 6		€3 6 . 1 9	
+ €1 7 . 2 0		+ €3 9 . 5 5		+ €1 9 . 4 3		+ €3 8 . 2 9		+ €1 4 . 5 9	

11.	€2 . 8 8	12.	€6 . 7 3	13.	€4 . 3 8	14.	€5 . 1 9	15.	€4 . 7 6
x	3	x	5	x	7	x	6	x	4

16.	6 4	17.	3 7	18.	4 5	19.	2 9	20.	3 4
x 1 6		x 2 8		x 1 7		x 1 9		x 1 7	

21.	2 7 7	22.	4 0 9	23.	3 2 8	24.	7 2 2	25.	3 4 5
+ 2 3 7		+ 3 8 8		+ 2 9 4		+ 1 7 9		+ 4 6 7	
– 3 9 9		– 3 7 8		– 1 4 6		– 5 1 7		– 6 6 6	

Unit 28 - Problems

A Figure it out.

1. How many wheels on 16 bicycles? ⬚
2. Bananas are 3 for 50c or 20c each. How much for 7 bananas? € ⬚
3. An aeroplane had 178 seats. Half the seats were used. How many seats were free? ⬚
4. Jill had €3·58 in her purse. She spent €1·27. How much has she now? € ⬚
5. Joe had 18 jellies and ate 3. He shared the rest with 2 friends. How many did each get? ⬚
6. A shopkeeper sold 27 newspapers. He had 44 left. How many had he at first? ⬚
7. Dad bought 4 pizzas and cut each in 8 portions. How many portions is that? ⬚
8. $\frac{1}{10}$ of a set of 100 Christmas lights do not work. How many lights work? ⬚
9. School begins at 8:50 a.m. Break is 1 hr 30 mins later. Break begins at ⬚ : ⬚ a.m.
10. Jane is 3 years older than Ann. Together their age is 15. What age is Jane? ⬚

B Think it out. Tick (✓) the correct answer.

1. How many €2·20 cinema tickets can you buy for €11·00? a 4 b 5 c 6
2. 71 people are on a bus. 34 are upstairs. How many are downstairs?
   a 35 b 37 c 47
3. Lunchtime is from 12:50 p.m. to 1:25 p.m. How long is lunchtime?
   a 25 mins b 45 mins c 35 mins
4. Chickens are €3·99 each. How much for 4 chickens? a €12·98 b €15·96 c €16·04
5. How many 9s in 57? a 6 b 7 c 8

6. The sides of a triangle are 7 cm, 4 cm and 6 cm. How long is the perimeter?
   a 8·5 cm b 17 cm c 34 cm
7. By how much is 34·5 less than 37·3?
   a 2·2 b 3·2 c 2·8
8. Jim did 25 sums each day for 5 days. How many was that? a 125 b 75 c 30
9. What is missing? 133 – 22 ⬚ 10 x 12
   a > b < c =
10. A ribbon was 3·6 m long. How long is $\frac{1}{4}$ of the ribbon? a 0·9 m b 7·6 m c 14·4 m

C Puzzle it out. Complete the Sudoku using 1, 2, 3, 4, 5, 6, 7 8 and 9 in each square, row and column.

Remember! Use each number only once in each square, row and column.

		2		9		3	6	4
	5	6	3		7			
1			2			5		
	9	5			1		2	
		3	7	2		9		
		1	4			8		6
				1	2			5
	2	7			6	1	8	
9		8		7		6		

114

Unit 28 - Check-up

A Tables

1. 9 x 6 = [ ]
2. 7 x 8 = [ ]
3. 36 ÷ 9 = [ ]
4. 28 ÷ [ ] = 4
5. 8 + 9 = [ ]
6. 72 ÷ [ ] = 9
7. 7 x [ ] = 28
8. [ ] x 9 = 54
9. 7 x 8 = [ ]
10. 9 x [ ] = 81

Score [ ]

B Computation

1.		6	0	8	2.			8	7	3.			3	7	4.	€3	9	·0	5	5.			2	6	1
	−	4	6	9		x			6			2		8		€2	7	·6	8		+	3	8	0
											+		3	0	+	€1	8	·4	9					
											7	8	5								−	4	0	6

Give yourself 2 marks for each correct sum. Score [ ]

C Fractions and Decimals... Tick (✓) the correct answer.

1. 4·6 + 1·9 =   a 5·15 b 5·3 c 6·5
2. 2·4 − 0·8 =   a 1·6 b 2·4 c 3·2
3. $\frac{3}{4}$ of 12 =   a 3 b 6 c 9
4. $\frac{1}{4}$ of 32 =   a 4 b 7 c 8
5. $\frac{1}{8}$ of 16 =   a 2 b 4 c 8

6. 0·5 + 2 − 0·2 =   a 2·3 b 2·8 c 3·3
7. 0·6 + 3·3 − 1 =   a 2·9 b 3·9 c 4·9
8. 1·5 − 0·2 + 1·3 =   a 1·6 b 2·4 c 2·6
9. 2·3 − 0·2 + 2 =   a 0·5 b 4·1 c 4·5
10. $\frac{1}{10}$ of 63 =   a 5·3 b 6·3 c 53

Score [ ]

D Shapes, Measures and Data... Write the times that are 25 minutes later than the times shown.

1. 10:05   [:]
2. 11:20   [:]
3. 8:55   [:]
4. 3:45   [:]
5. 4:40   [:]
6. 1:20   [:]
7. 12:35   [:]
8. 7:40   [:]
9. 9:10   [:]
10. 1:15   [:]

Score [ ]

E Problem Solving

1. A bus travels at 30 km an hour. How far will it travel in 1 hr 30 mins?   [ ] km
2. $\frac{2}{5}$ of the 50 children on a tour are boys. How many is that?   [ ]
3. I walked 2·5 km, 3·6 km and 3·1 km this week. How much is that in total?   [ ] km
4. I paid €4·40 for a toy and sold it for a quarter more. What profit did I make?   € [ ]
5. Biros are 35c each or 3 for €1. How much for 8 biros?   € [ ]

Give yourself 2 marks for each correct answer. Score [ ]

A Tables

1. $9 + 8 =$ ☐
2. $7 +$ ☐ $= 14$
3. $17 -$ ☐ $= 10$
4. $19 -$ ☐ $= 9$
5. $8 +$ ☐ $= 13$
6. $9 \times 6 =$ ☐
7. $9 \times$ ☐ $= 81$
8. $4 \times$ ☐ $= 36$
9. $48 \div 6 =$ ☐
10. $49 \div$ ☐ $= 7$
11. $63 \div$ ☐ $= 7$
12. $60 \div 6 =$ ☐

B Calculate.

1. $44 + 31 + 29 =$ ☐
2. $487 - 28 =$ ☐
3. $356 + 426 =$ ☐
4. $207 +$ ☐ $= 429$
5. $686 -$ ☐ $= 104$
6. $(231 \times 2) + 3 =$ ☐
7. $(56 \div 8) \times 2 =$ ☐
8. $251 + 136 + 144 =$ ☐
9. $502 + 133 + 20 =$ ☐
10. $385 + 122 =$ ☐
11. €2·43 $\times$ ☐ $=$ €4·86
12. €3·13 $\times$ ☐ $=$ €9·39

C Numbers... Complete the tables.

Tables	12	16	18	24	30	32	36	40	42	48
÷ 3		—				—		—		
÷ 4			—		—				—	
÷ 6		—				—		—		
÷ 8	—		—		—		—		—	

D Data... There are 24 children in Miss Murphy's fourth class. Complete the information table.

1.	Half have blue eyes. How many is that?	
2.	One-third have brown eyes. How many is that?	
3.	The others have green eyes. How many is that?	
4.	One-third are boys. How many is that?	
5.	How many girls are in the class?	
6.	Two-thirds of the class are 9 years old. How many is that?	
7.	Half of the boys walk to school. How many is that?	
8.	One-sixth of the class have a bicycle. How many is that?	
9.	The girls brought €2 each to school. How much is that?	
10.	One-quarter of the class play football after school. How many is that?	
11.	5 girls and half the boys have a dog. How many is that?	
12.	One-eighth of the class was absent yesterday. How many is that?	

E Figure it out. Use $+$, $-$, $\times$ or $\div$ to complete the number sentences.

1. $(9$ ☐ $3)$ ☐ $4 = 7$
2. $(24$ ☐ $3)$ ☐ $2 = 10$
3. $(8$ ☐ $5)$ ☐ $2 = 6$
4. $(9$ ☐ $3)$ ☐ $4 = 12$
5. $(9$ ☐ $2)$ ☐ $5 = 35$
6. $(11$ ☐ $4)$ ☐ $1 = 43$
7. 10 ☐ 5 ☐ $2 = 100$
8. $(2$ ☐ $3)$ ☐ $2 = 8$
9. $(2·5$ ☐ $2)$ ☐ $1 = 4$
10. $3·5$ ☐ $1·5$ ☐ $2·5 = 4·5$
11. (€3·50 ☐ €2·50) ☐ $2 =$ €2·00
12. €7·65 ☐ €5·56 $=$ €13·21

Be careful! Some division sums have remainders.

A Work it out.

1.		4	5
x			
3	1	5	

2.		2	6
x			
2	0	8	

3.		3	9
x			
2	7	3	

4.		6	2
x			
5	5	8	

5.		3	3
x			
2	3	1	

6.
```
      4
  2   5
+   7 6
  6 7 8
```

7.
```
    3 7
  1   4
+ 3 2
  5 7 8
```

8.
```
    2 7
    5 8
+ 2   1
  7 2 5
```

9.
```
    2 3
  1   4
+   3 8
  5 0 6
```

10.
```
    2 4
  1   7
+ 2 6
  7 6 3
```

11.		7	1
x	4	5	

12.		7	8
x	2	6	

13.		4	9
x	3	3	

14.		9	7
x	6	2	

15.		6	4
x	4	3	

16. 3 | €6 ·3 6

17. 4 | €8 ·0 4

18. 6 | €6 ·1 8

19. 5 | €6 ·5 5

20. 9 | €9 ·8 1

B Work it out.

1. 8 | 9 2 5

2. 7 | 3 2 8

3. 9 | 4 1 2

4. 6 | 3 0 5

5. 4 | 5 2 6

6.	hrs	mins
	1	3 5
+	2	4 0

7.	hrs	mins
	1	4 0
+	1	2 0

8.	hrs	mins
	1	3 5
+	2	5 0

9.	hrs	mins
	1	3 0
+	2	5 5

10.	hrs	mins
	1	1 0
+	2	1 5

(R for 1-5)

11.
```
  3 4 ·5
- 1 7 ·2
```

12.
```
  4 0 ·7
- 1 8 ·9
```

13.
```
  2 7 ·2
- 1 9 ·3
```

14.
```
  3 5 ·4
- 1 9 ·5
```

15.
```
  2 9 ·6
- 1 1 ·8
```

16.
```
  €9 5 ·4 8
- €6 6 ·1 9
```

17.
```
  €6 2 ·4 7
- €3 5 ·2 8
```

18.
```
  €7 4 ·1 9
- €5 3 ·3 2
```

19.
```
  €6 3 ·2 7
- €4 4 ·3 5
```

20.
```
  €6 2 ·2 2
- €5 6 ·6 5
```

21.		4	5
x	3	6	

22.		2	3
x	4	7	

23.		4	4
x	2	8	

24.		7	2
x	5	3	

25.		2	9
x	5	4	

Unit 29 - Problems

A **Figure it out. There are 32 children in 4th class.**

1. 11 of the children are boys. How many are girls? ▢
2. $\frac{1}{2}$ of the children go to school by car. How many is that? ▢
3. $\frac{1}{4}$ of the children walk to school. How many is that? ▢
4. The others travel on the school bus. How many is that? ▢
5. $\frac{1}{3}$ of the girls have blue eyes. How many is that? ▢
6. $\frac{1}{2}$ of the children drink milk at school. 5 are girls. How many are boys? ▢
7. The 15-minute morning break begins at 10:30 a.m. When does it end? ▢ : ▢ a.m.
8. The class has triplets and two sets of twins. How many children is that? ▢
9. 5 boys and $\frac{1}{3}$ of the girls love football. How many do not like football? ▢
10. Today 4 children are absent. 2 are girls. How many boys are at school? ▢

B **Think it out. Tick (✓) the correct answer.**

1. 3 bags weigh 1·75 kg, 1·50 kg and 2·25 kg. What is the total weight?
   a 4·5 kg b 5·25 kg c 5·5 kg

2. $\frac{3}{10}$ of the 70 people at a match are children. How many is that? a 13 b 21 c 30

3. A film began at 7:15 p.m. and ended at 8:35 p.m. How long was it?
   a 70 mins b 75 mins c 80 mins

4. Lucky Bags are €1·15 each or 6 for €6·50. How much for 8 bags?
   a €7·65 b €8·80 c €9·20

5. How many boxes of 6 eggs can be filled from 78 eggs? a 13 b 14 c 15

6. What is the perimeter of a rectangle if the sides are 8 cm and 5 cm?
   a 13 cm b 18 cm c 26 cm

7. By how much is 81·4 greater than 74·9?
   a 6·5 b 7·5 c 8·3

8. A €36 toy was reduced by one-third. What is the new price? a €12 b €24 c €48

9. What is missing?
   (7 x 8) + 1 ▢ (8 x 10) − 5
   a > b < c =

10. Miss Stamp teaches $\frac{1}{3}$ of the 69 pupils in a school. How many is that?
    a 13 b 23 c 31

C **Puzzle it out. Do the sums and use the answers to crack the code.**

R	858	M	924	C	621	I	864	S	855	N	651	U	252	G	342	E	256	O	448

If you need to, you can work out these sums in your copy.

1. 45 x 19 = ▢
2. 18 x 14 = ▢
3. 42 x 22 = ▢
4. 84 x 11 = ▢
5. 16 x 16 = ▢
6. 33 x 26 = ▢
7. 54 x 16 = ▢
8. 57 x 15 = ▢
9. 27 x 23 = ▢
10. 28 x 16 = ▢
11. 44 x 21 = ▢
12. 96 x 9 = ▢
13. 31 x 21 = ▢
14. 19 x 18 = ▢

Sum No.	1	2	3	4	5	6		7	8		9	10	11	12	13	14
Answer																
Code																

Unit 29 - Check-up

A Tables

1. 8 + ☐ = 14
2. 8 – ☐ = 5
3. 17 – ☐ = 8
4. ☐ – 10 = 6
5. 3 x 6 = ☐
6. ☐ x 6 = 42
7. ☐ x 8 = 56
8. 54 ÷ ☐ = 9
9. ☐ ÷ 3 = 7
10. ☐ ÷ 8 = 5

Score ☐

B Computation

1.		1	3	7
		4	7	7
	+	2	0	6

2.	hrs	mins
	1	4 5
	2	2 0

3.		7	8
	x	3	9

4.	€4 1 ·8 0
	– €1 9 ·9 3
	+ €2 8 ·1 7

5.		4	8
	x	1	7
3			

Give yourself 2 marks for each correct sum.

Score ☐

C Fractions and Decimals

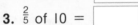

1. $\frac{3}{10}$ of 100 = ☐
2. $\frac{1}{3}$ of 24 = ☐
3. $\frac{2}{5}$ of 10 = ☐
4. 4·6 + 0·3 + 3·7 = ☐
5. 5·5 – 1·2 + 0·7 = ☐

6. 4·2 + 1·2 – 1·3 = ☐
7. 2·5 – 1·3 + 1·3 = ☐
8. 1·9 + 0·5 + 1·6 = ☐
9. $\frac{1}{6}$ of 18 less $\frac{1}{6}$ of 6 = ☐
10. $\frac{3}{4}$ of 4 plus $\frac{1}{2}$ of 10 = ☐

Score ☐

D Shapes, Measures and Data... Ring the number or amount that does not belong.

1. 1·5, 1$\frac{1}{2}$, $\frac{3}{4}$
2. 33 cm, 33c, €0·33
3. 1·25 m, 125 cm, 1·25 km
4. 130 secs, 1$\frac{1}{2}$ mins, 90 sec
5. 0·2 kg, 200 kg, $\frac{1}{5}$ kg
6. 750 ml, 1·75 l, 0·75 l
7. 89c, €0·89, 0·89 cm
8. $\frac{3}{4}$, 1$\frac{1}{2}$, $\frac{6}{8}$
9. 0·3 kg, 30 g, 300 g
10. $\frac{7}{10}$, 0·07, 0·7

Score ☐

E Problem Solving... Tick (✓) the correct answer.

1. How many 9s in 86?   a 7   b 8   c 9
2. How many grams in 1·5 kg?   a 15 g   b 150 g   c 1500 g
3. By how much is 6·7 less than 8·4?   a 1·3   b 1·7   c 2·3
4. What is missing? 33 ÷ 3 ▨ 36 ÷ 3 =   a <   b =   c >
5. How much for 11 tickets at 12c each?   a €1·21   b €1·23   c €1·32

Give yourself 2 marks for each correct answer.

Score ☐

A Tables

1. 8 x ☐ = 64   **4.** ☐ x 6 = 54   **7.** 63 ÷ ☐ = 7   **10.** 63 ÷ ☐ = 9

2. ☐ x 9 = 81   **5.** 9 x ☐ = 27   **8.** ☐ ÷ 8 = 7   **11.** 72 ÷ 8 = ☐

3. 10 x ☐ = 60   **6.** 7 x ☐ = 42   **9.** 56 ÷ ☐ = 8   **12.** ☐ ÷ 9 = 9

B Calculate.

1. 274 + 123 − 20 = ☐   **5.** 148 − 55 = ☐   **9.** 2·5 + 2·5 − 1 = ☐

2. 475 − 11 + 35 = ☐   **6.** 101 x 6 = ☐   **10.** 3 − 0·5 + 2·5 = ☐

3. 208 + 133 = ☐   **7.** 168 ÷ 4 = ☐   **11.** 34·5 + ☐ = 50

4. 633 + 244 − 32 = ☐   **8.** €11·66 − €2·43 = € ☐   **12.** 25 − ☐ = 12.5

C Numbers... Are these numbers > (greater than), < (less than) or = (equal to) each other?

1. $\frac{1}{5}$ of 15 ☐ $\frac{1}{2}$ of 6   **5.** (7 x 4) − 2 ☐ 5 x 5   **9.** 12 x 6 ☐ 8 x 9

2. $\frac{1}{2}$ of 8 ☐ $\frac{1}{4}$ of 12   **6.** (5 x 6) + 3 ☐ 3 x 11   **10.** 1 − 0·3 ☐ 1 − 0·4

3. $\frac{1}{6}$ of 12 ☐ $\frac{1}{3}$ of 9   **7.** (25 ÷ 5) x 4 ☐ 2 x 12   **11.** 0·25 + 0·5 ☐ 1 − 0·5

4. $\frac{1}{4}$ of 16 ☐ $\frac{1}{2}$ of 8   **8.** 2·7 + 2·3 ☐ 3 + 3   **12.** €18·90 ÷ 3 ☐ €5·00 + €1·00

D Data... There are 30 children in Mr Brown's fourth class. Complete the information table.

1.	One-tenth have red hair. How many is that?	
2.	One-sixth have fair hair. How many is that?	
3.	Half have brown hair. How many is that?	
4.	The others have black hair. How many is that?	
5.	Two-thirds of the class are girls. How many is that?	
6.	One-quarter of the girls are aged 9. How many is that?	
7.	Half of the girls walk to school. How many is that?	
8.	One-fifth of the boys cycle to school. How many is that?	
9.	One-third of the class travel on the bus. How many is that?	
10.	Half of the boys play hurling. How many is that?	
11.	Three-quarters of the girls go swimming. How many is that?	
12.	One-tenth of the class was absent yesterday. How many is that?	

E Figure it out. Use +, −, X or ÷ to complete the number sentences.

1. (6 ☐ 3) ☐ 2 = 6   **5.** 7 ☐ 2 = 3·5   **9.** 5 ☐ 5 ☐ 2 = 50

2. (9 ☐ 3) ☐ 1 = 7   **6.** (25 ☐ 2) ☐ 10 = 40   **10.** 2·5 ☐ 2·5 ☐ 1 = 4

3. (15 ☐ 3) ☐ 2 = 10   **7.** (16 ☐ 4) ☐ 3 = 7   **11.** 4 ☐ 3 ☐ 2 = 24

4. (7 ☐ 7) ☐ 1 = 50   **8.** 2$\frac{1}{2}$ ☐ 1 ☐ $\frac{1}{2}$ = 3   **12.** (100 ☐ 10) ☐ 2 = 8

A Work it out.

1.	2.	3.	4.	5.
9 4	4 7	8 9	6 7	8 9
× 8	× 7	× 6	× 9	× 4

6.
```
      0
  3   9
+   8 8
  8 2 3
```

7.
```
    2     7
  1 0 4
+ 3 5
  6 6 6
```

8.
```
    4 3
  5 8
+     1
  5 3 4
```

9.
```
    2 3
        4
+   3 8
  4 3 8
```

10.
```
      2 5
  1   8
+ 3 0
  8 9 9
```

11. 4)€6·84   12. 9)€9·54   13. 6)€6·72   14. 8)€8·48   15. 7)€9·45

16.
```
    4 1 9
+ 1 0 5

- 3 7 7
```

17.
```
    2 8 9
+ 3 9 2

- 4 1 1
```

18.
```
    4 0 3
+ 2 5 0

- 1 0 7
```

19.
```
    5 0 4
+     9 9

- 3 5 0
```

20.
```
    4 1 7
+     7 4

- 2 8 8
```

B Work it out.

1. 9)6 8 7   2. 7)4 7 8   3. 8)2 7 6   4. 6)3 0 2   5. 9)1 5 9
(R)

6.
m	cm
1	3 0
2	2 5
+ 1	1 0

7.
m	cm
2	3 5
1	7 0
+ 2	2 5

8.
m	cm
1	2 8
1	3 4
+ 1	7 0

9.
m	cm
4	2 6
3	1 5
+ 2	1 0

10.
m	cm
2	2 5
1	1 5
+ 2	2 0

11.
```
    2 6
×   2 4
```

12.
```
    5 4
× 1 8
```

13.
```
    3 4
× 1 6
```

14.
```
    3 6
× 4 2
```

15.
```
    8 0
× 2 2
```

16.
```
  €9 4·1 8
− €8 8·2 7
```

17.
```
  €4 0·0 9
− €1 7·2 0
```

18.
```
  €7 9·2 5
− €2 1·6 0
```

19.
```
  €1 3·2 8
−   €4·3 5
```

20.
```
  €6 6·4 5
− €3 4·3 0
```

Unit 30 - Problems

A Creating problems is fun! Create 10 maths problems based on school events such as a school tour, sports day, book fair or cake sale. **Be sure your answers are correct!**

Here are some sample questions:

1. 20 children paid €1·20 each to go on a school tour. How much did they pay altogether?

€ ☐

2. The buns in a cake sale were 30c each. Tom bought 7 buns. How much did he pay?

€ ☐

3. The teacher was selling books. How much for 3 books costing €3·40, €1·55 and €2·20?

€ ☐

1. _____

_____ Answer: ☐

2. _____

_____ Answer: ☐

3. _____

_____ Answer: ☐

4. _____

_____ Answer: ☐

5. _____

_____ Answer: ☐

6. _____

_____ Answer: ☐

7. _____

_____ Answer: ☐

8. _____

_____ Answer: ☐

9. _____

_____ Answer: ☐

10. _____

_____ Answer: ☐

B Pick your best 3 questions and see if your friends can get the correct answer.

C Draw pictures for three of your questions.

Unit 30 - Check-up

A Tables

1. $5 \times 8 =$ [ ] 4. $19 - 10 =$ [ ] 7. [ ] $\div 2 = 7$ 10. $72 \div 8 =$ [ ]

2. $9 \times$ [ ] $= 81$ 5. $13 -$ [ ] $= 4$ 8. [ ] $\div 5 = 8$

3. $8 \times 7 =$ [ ] 6. [ ] $- 6 = 8$ 9. [ ] $\div 5 = 9$

Score [ ]

B Computation

1.		4	1	9	2.			7	1	4	3.	kg		g		4.	€1	8	·2	3	5.		6	8	9
						x				9		1	1	8	0	−		€8	·9	9		−	3	9	8
	+	1	7	7								1	1	4	5										
		9	2	2								+	2	0	0	5	x			9		−	2	0	7

Give yourself 2 marks for each correct sum.

Score [ ]

C Fractions and Decimals... Ring the correct amount.

1.	0·2	🏠🏠🏠🏠🏠🏠🏠🏠🏠🏠	6.	$\frac{1}{5}$	☺☺☺☺☺☺☺☺☺☺
2.	0·4	❤❤❤❤❤❤❤❤❤❤	7.	0·6	✦✦✦✦✦✦✦✦✦✦
3.	$\frac{1}{3}$	👂👂👂👂👂👂👂👂👂👂	8.	0·33	🚲🚲🚲🚲🚲🚲🚲🚲🚲🚲
4.	0·25	⛳⛳⛳⛳⛳⛳⛳⛳	9.	$\frac{1}{6}$	🚚🚚🚚🚚🚚🚚🚚🚚🚚🚚🚚🚚
5.	0·75	🚗🚗🚗🚗🚗🚗🚗🚗🚗🚗🚗🚗	10.	$\frac{2}{3}$	🎗🎗🎗🎗🎗🎗🎗🎗🎗

Score [ ]

D Shapes, Measures and Data

Answer the questions.

1. How many €0·75 buns can I buy with €5·00? [ ]

2. If the buns are 3 for €2·00, how many €0·75 buns can I buy for €4·75? [ ]

Which measure is greater:

3. kilogram or gram? [ ]

4. millilitre or litre? [ ]

5. centimetre or kilometre? [ ]

Give yourself 2 marks for each correct answer.

Score [ ]

E Problem Solving

Granny has an orchard with 14 apple trees, 8 pear trees and 6 plum trees. Half of the pear trees grow beside the wall. The plum trees each had 20 plums this year. Granny used one-third of all the plums to make jam. Half of the apple trees have small red apples.

1. How many trees altogether are in the orchard? [ ]

2. How many pear trees grow beside the wall? [ ]

3. How many plums in total came from the plum trees this year? [ ]

4. How many plums did Granny use for jam? [ ]

5. How many apple trees have small red apples? [ ]

Give yourself 2 marks for each correct answer.

Score [ ]

Shapes and Measures

Shapes: 2-dimensional or *flat*

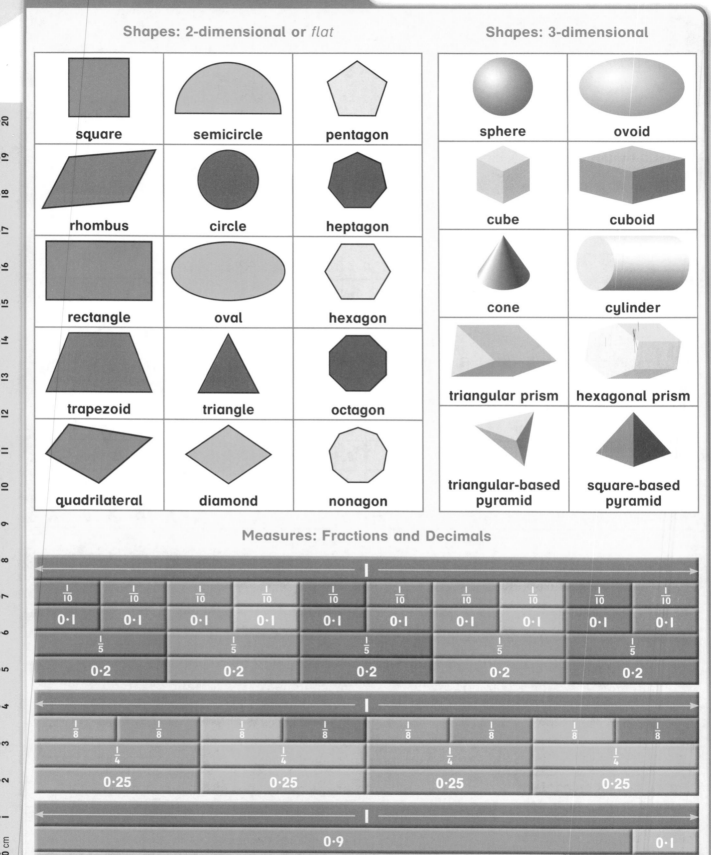

square	semicircle	pentagon
rhombus	circle	heptagon
rectangle	oval	hexagon
trapezoid	triangle	octagon
quadrilateral	diamond	nonagon

Shapes: 3-dimensional

sphere	ovoid
cube	cuboid
cone	cylinder
triangular prism	hexagonal prism
triangular-based pyramid	square-based pyramid

Measures: Fractions and Decimals

124

Measures: Length – km / m / cm / mm

I kilometre	=	1000 metres
I metre	=	100 centimetres
I centimetre	=	10 millimetres

Measures: Weight – kg / g

I kilogram	=	1000 grams
$\frac{1}{2}$ or 0·5 kg	=	500 g
$\frac{1}{4}$ or 0·25 kg	=	250 g
$\frac{1}{10}$ or 0·1 kg	=	100 g

Measures: Capacity – l / ml

I litre	=	1000 millilitres
$\frac{1}{2}$ or 0·5 l	=	500 ml
$\frac{1}{4}$ or 0·25 l	=	250 ml
$\frac{1}{10}$ or 0·1 l	=	100 ml

Measures: Time

I year	= 365 days = 52 weeks + I day
I week	= 7 days
I day	= 24 hours
I hour	= 60 minutes
I minute	= 60 seconds

Word Power

Maths is easier when words make sense. Here are some interesting word parts:

bi- → 2, tri- → 3, quad- → 4, semi- → $\frac{1}{2}$, deci- → $\frac{1}{10}$, cent- → 100, multi- → many,
circ- → around, para- → alongside, temp- → heat, peri- → going around, fract → break

bicycle	two-wheeled vehicle	**multi**ply	many additions: $3 + 3 + 3 + 3 = 4 \times 3$
binocular	two viewing eyes	multi-**storey**	many levels, such as in a car park
bisect	cut in two parts	**circ**le	shape that goes around
tricycle	three-wheeled vehicle	**circ**us	large round theatre or tent
triangle	three-angled shape	**circ**umference	measure around a circle
triceratops	three-horned dinosaur	**para**llel lines	lines exactly alongside ══
quad bike	four-wheeled vehicle	**para**llelogram	4-sided shape with parallel lines
quadrilateral	four-sided shape	**temp**erature	measure of heat
semicircle	half a circle	**temp**er	getting heated, getting cross
semi-detached	a house attached to another on one side (half)	**fract**ion	a number broken into parts: $\frac{1}{4}$, $\frac{3}{4}$
decimal	tenth parts of 1: 0·1, 0·2, 0·5	**fract**ure	a break, such as a fractured arm
centipede	insect with 100 parts	**fract**ious	a break up, row or argument
centimetre	$\frac{1}{100}$ of a metre measure	**peri**meter	length around the edge
centigrade	$\frac{1}{100}$ of a heat measure	**peri**winkle	small circular seashell

My Profile

Struggling (1–3)	Fair (4–6)	Well Done (7–9)	Star Performer (10)

Tables

10																														
9																														
8																														
7																														
6																														
5																														
4																														
3																														
2																														
1																														
Unit	1	2	3	4	5	6	7	8	9	10	11	12	13	14	15	16	17	18	19	20	21	22	23	24	25	26	27	28	29	30

Computation

10																														
9																														
8																														
7																														
6																														
5																														
4																														
3																														
2																														
1																														
Unit	1	2	3	4	5	6	7	8	9	10	11	12	13	14	15	16	17	18	19	20	21	22	23	24	25	26	27	28	29	30

Fractions and Decimals

10																														
9																														
8																														
7																														
6																														
5																														
4																														
3																														
2																														
1																														
Unit	1	2	3	4	5	6	7	8	9	10	11	12	13	14	15	16	17	18	19	20	21	22	23	24	25	26	27	28	29	30

Struggling (1–3)	Fair (4–6)	Well Done (7–9)	Star Performer (10)

Shapes, Measures and Data

10																														
9																														
8																														
7																														
6																														
5																														
4																														
3																														
2																														
1																														
Unit	1	2	3	4	5	6	7	8	9	10	11	12	13	14	15	16	17	18	19	20	21	22	23	24	25	26	27	28	29	30

Problem Solving

10																														
9																														
8																														
7																														
6																														
5																														
4																														
3																														
2																														
1																														
Unit	1	2	3	4	5	6	7	8	9	10	11	12	13	14	15	16	17	18	19	20	21	22	23	24	25	26	27	28	29	30

Comments

Term 1: _____

_____

_____ Date: _____

Term 2: _____

_____

_____ Date: _____

Term 3: _____

_____

_____ Date: _____

Table Crackers

Learn your tables and become a table wizard! See how the numbers work together.
What patterns can you spot?